AN ALASKAN
ADVENTURE

A TRAVELOGUE
AND ENVIRONMENTAL TREATISE

ALAN R. ADASCHIK

ALASKAN ADVENTURE

A Travelogue and Environmental Treatise

ALAN R. ADASCHIK

ISBN: 978-1-967375-80-6 (Paperback)
ISBN: 978-1-967375-83-7 (Hardback)
ISBN: 978-1-967375-81-3 (E-book)

Library of Congress Control Number: 2025919339

Printed in the United States of America

Published by:

info@thequippyquill.com
(302) 295-2278

Contents

Introduction

All my life, I have dreamed about visiting Alaska. My longing stems from my perception that Alaska is America's last frontier and last bastion of freedom, as freedom was known to the pioneers. As a teenager growing up in Brooklyn, New York, I believed the world was much too crowded. Please don't get me wrong, I like people. When you talk to one, they become a person, and the experience is usually quite pleasant. On the other hand, how many people around do you need to be happy: ten, twenty, one hundred, five hundred? Whatever the number, everyone else is excess baggage that gets in your way at traffic lights, makes you wait for tables in restaurants, and detracts from your overall quality of life.

Someday, I want to get a bumper sticker that reads, *People Are Pollution*. True, they are and can be many other things, but after all is said and done, each person born makes a small but measurable contribution to an overcrowded and polluted world. Therefore, while the arrival of a new baby is a great joy to those with a personal attachment to it, it is a detriment to everyone else who must suffer the consequences of this new presence. I suppose this is why I didn't get married for the first time until I was thirty-three years old and never cared much about having any children of my own.

This book is a travelogue of my trip to Alaska taken with my wife Gayle, and our two Schnauzers, Scooter and Sally. I apologize for starting out with an editorial, but my comments set the backdrop for our journey.

I love the great outdoors and the solitude it offers. As far as America is concerned, outdoors and solitude are what Alaska is all about. Therefore, retired and at the ripe old age of fifty-eight, Gayle and I purchased a thirty-seven-foot motor home to make the journey in a grand and glorious style. What a beauty! She has all the latest technology, including two push-button slide-outs that turn our bus-like traveling quarters into a roomy country cottage. Motor homes have come a long way in the past several years, and those not familiar with the latest advances have no idea how spacious and comfortable they are.

Being a novice at RV'ing, the thought of towing a car behind us did not appeal to me. I didn't want to deal with not being able to back up and the other drawbacks associated with a towed vehicle. Therefore, for area transportation, we settled upon a rear bumper-mounted 650cc dirt bike, set up for both on and off-road use. I reasoned that if the weather was bad, I didn't want to be touring anyway, and a dirt bike would allow Gayle and me to see places unreachable by a conventional four-wheel vehicle or even a restricted road motorcycle. We also have two folding bicycles and an inflatable kayak.

After gearing up and outfitting our freedom machine, we took several short trips to become familiar with its equipment and to ensure we were ready for our Alaskan adventure. On these foray's we met other people who had visited Alaska and to our dismay, were told that bringing a new motor home to there is foolish because of the poor road conditions. Broken radiators, chipped windshields, and shredded tires are a routine occurrence.

We were committed to our journey, and having no other choice, I improvised a padded bra to protect our RV's front end. I also considered mounting a small seat, just below the windshield. I reasoned that Gayle could sit upon it with a catcher's mitt and catch stones that pop up off the road. This would probably work well, provided she stays alert and I do not hit the brakes too hard. For some reason, Gayle shot this idea down. I guess I will never understand women.

Gayle and I live in Florida and left the state in early spring to visit friends and family in the New York/New England area before departing for Alaska. After doing so, we headed west to visit family in Michigan and Indiana. We are now in Indiana, and it is here that the log of our journey will begin.

CHAPTER 1

The Northern Plains

Sunday, July 7, writing from LaPorte, Indiana

That's it for relatives for a while. Tomorrow, we leave for Alaska and begin our adventure. We will travel over three thousand five hundred miles during the next few weeks, just getting there. Gayle's goal is to pan for gold and find a flake or two. I'm a little more ambitious. I want to find a woolly mammoth frozen in a glacier. I am sure mammoth meat must be very tasty because of how long it has been aged. I can hardly wait to sink my choppers into a five-thousand-year-old chunk of hindquarter. Talk about a meal that spans ages.

We also plan to fish for halibut. I didn't know much about this fish before planning our journey and was intrigued to learn that they are a huge flounder. The record halibut, caught commercially, weighed over nine hundred pounds.

Saturday, July 13, writing from Miles City, Montana

Miles City, Montana

Hoping to get through the Chicago area before rush hour, we left La Porte, Indiana, on Monday at five in the morning. This was not early enough. It took three hours to travel ninety miles. Talk about overpopulation! The traffic finally opened up on the other side of town, and as planned, we picked up I-94 and headed north for Wisconsin. We decided to take I-94 in lieu of I-90 because it is closer to Canada and I thought that this would be the more scenic route.

Wisconsin is famous for its dairy products. However, it is also a progressive state that led the way to direct primary elections, the regulation of public utilities, pensions for teachers, the establishment of kindergartens, minimum-wage laws, and workers' compensation. It was also the first state to abolish the death penalty and has been a leader in the development of farmers' institutes, farm cooperatives, dairy farmers' associations, and cheese-making federations. One of the nation's first hydroelectric plants was built in Wisconsin, and it was the first state to adopt the number system for marking highways. It was the first state to pass a law mandating safety belts in all new automobiles bought in the state, and Wisconsin played a major role in establishing the Republican Party.

As we drove through Wisconsin, picturesque farms and rolling hills dominated the scenery. Monday evening, we stayed at a state park in the town of Hudson, just shy of the Minnesota Border. The park was beautiful, and our campsite was about a hundred yards from a lakeside beach. Breaking out our folding bicycles, we followed a trail around the lake and were delighted when we came upon a dam with a fifty-foot waterfall. Two teenage boys were fishing in the pond at the bottom of the dam, and it was a nostalgic scene, like something out of Huckleberry Finn.

Tuesday, we woke up to cloudy skies. We crossed the Minnesota border and took the I-694 bypass around Minneapolis/St. Paul, enduring heavy showers as we traveled. We were once again caught in rush hour traffic, but not as bad as Chicago. Minnesota is much the same as Wisconsin; farms and rolling hills. I am sure there are really beautiful places in both these states, but you do not see much from an interstate highway.

Minnesota possesses some of the nation's richest farmland, which helps establish the state as a leading producer of milk products, corn, hogs, soybeans, and wheat. The state is also rife with scenic beauty, and its sparkling lakes and deep pine woods make it a vacation wonderland. Minnesota is blessed with a plethora of game animals and fish that are a major attraction for outdoorsmen from all over the nation. Its numerous lakes and extensive woodlands also are an attraction to campers, canoeists, and hikers.

We drove through Minnesota, crossed into North Dakota and stopped for the night in Jamestown, a town on the James River. We chose Jamestown as a stopping place because their campground included a restaurant on its grounds. Jamestown is famous for its buffalo museum and a three-story tall statue of a buffalo that can be seen from I-94.

Gayle was anxious to see a real buffalo, so we planned on doing so before we left the following day. Unfortunately, the local buffalo were hidden behind a fence, and you had to pay to see them. I was offended by this, so to protest, we stole a peek through a hole we found in the fence. Seeing those buffalo as they were saddened me. They once owned the plains, with their herds stretching from horizon to horizon and now they have been reduced to being a cheap tourist attraction behind a restaurant in Jamestown. I had no reservation about leaving this place. Gayle wanted to spend another day there, which illustrates a universal truth of life and RV'ing; men always want to move on and women always want to stop and smell the roses.

On the road again in North Dakota we discovered why the plains are called "great". Finally, we are traveling somewhere visibly different from what we are used to seeing back east. "Rolling hills" does not adequately describe the panoramic vistas that unfolded before us. The hills were immense, with summits three to five miles apart. They were covered in grass, with a tree or two here and there to break up the monotony. Crossing the top of one hill, in the distance, you could see the top of the next; but even more spectacular was the view up and down the valley for several miles in both directions. The feeling of openness was breathtaking. For the first time in my life I know what is meant by wide open spaces and believe me, unless you see the Great Plains, you will never really know the true meaning of this expression.

North Dakota was named after the Sioux Indians who once lived here. The Sioux called themselves Dakota or Lakota, meaning allies or friends. The geographic center of North America lies in North Dakota and is near the town of Rugby in the north-central part of the state. The state is almost entirely covered by farms and ranches, with the chief crop being wheat. The state produces most of the nation's flaxseed, sunflower seeds, and barley. In addition to these crops the state also leads in the production of oats, pinto beans, rye, and sugar beets.

Few settlers came to North Dakota before the 1870's because railroads had not yet reached the area. However, this changed in the 1870's and with the advent of railroad transportation, large wheat-producing farms developed. The farms were highly profitable and became known as bonanza farms. The success of these farms attracted more settlers and the population of the state exploded by the turn of the century.

The rolling hills of North Dakota from I-94. The light brown dots on the side of the hill are huge rolls of hay.

Our goal for the day is to reach Medora, twenty-seven miles from the Montana border. We chose this town as a destination because its population is one hundred souls, and we had a choice of two reasonably priced RV parks. At the time, I never imagined the magical place we would find. As we approached Medora, hints of what was to come began to appear. Here and there were increasing numbers of curious piles of dirt, fifty to one hundred feet high. They looked like huge pimples or termite mounds. Finally, about three miles outside of Medora, someone threw a switch and changed the world; before us stood the Dakota Badlands.

Dumb struck, Gayle and I pulled over to gawk at the magnificent scenery. Recovering, we exited the interstate and drove a short distance to Medora. Medora turned out to be a small and picturesque western town, snuggled between cliffs of multi-colored rock and stone, which were punctuated by small trees and sagebrush. There are two levels of land in the area: the top which is flat and level and the bottom which is also flat and level. Separating the two are cliffs which are anything but flat and level.

Main Street, downtown in Medora, North Dakota

A picture of our shuttle craft, taken from a bluff overlooking our campground in Medora.

Medora was founded by the Marquis de Mores and named after his wife. The Marquis was no aristocratic pansy, but instead, one of the biggest ranchers in the area who built his own meat packing plant so he wouldn't have to ship his cattle to Chicago for processing. He was also a good friend of the young Teddy Roosevelt, who, until he was thirty, ranched nearby. Teddy had moved to the area as a youth for health reasons, and it was here that he began the legend that would one day propel him into the White House. Yesterday, Gayle and I toured Theodore Roosevelt National Park by motorcycle. The scenery took our breath away. The park looked like a set from a Hollywood movie. Of special delight was the herd of buffalo we encountered grazing freely within the park as God intended.

A herd of buffalo in Theodore Roosevelt National Park.

Theodore Roosevelt National Park's most outstanding feature is the scenic badlands along the Little Missouri River. It is here where water and wind have carved deep gullies and steep hills into the landscape. The park also includes a cattle ranch that President Theodore Roosevelt operated when he was in the area. A restored cabin where Teddy Roosevelt once lived is available for visitors to tour.

Teddy Roosevelt was an adventurer who believed in what he called the "strenuous life." He reveled in horseback riding, swimming, hunting, hiking, and boxing. His favorite expression was "bully", which today would translate into, "out of sight". Cartoonists had a field day with Roosevelt's rimless glasses, bushy mustache, prominent teeth, and jutting jaw. He was once portrayed as a bear cub, and picking up on this, toymakers were soon producing stuffed bears that are still known today as *teddy bears*.

Teddy Roosevelt became a national hero during the Spanish-American War in 1898, where he commanded the Rough Riders. This exposure enabled him to win the governorship of New York State, and two years later, he became Vice-President. Six months after taking office, President William McKinley was assassinated, and Roosevelt assumed the Presidency. In 1904, Roosevelt was elected President, and being a "trustbuster," he tirelessly worked to limit the power of corporations and big business. Toward this end, he spearheaded laws to regulate the railroads, protect people from harmful foods and drugs, and conserve the nation's forests and other natural resources.

Teddy Roosevelt was also no slouch in foreign affairs. The centerpiece of his foreign policy, as he put it, was to *speak softly and carry a big stick*. In this vein, he expanded the U.S. Navy, started construction of the Panama Canal, and kept European powers out of Latin America. While keeping the world's other imperialistic nations at bay, he also managed to become the first American to win the Nobel Peace Prize.

CHAPTER 2

The Road to Glacier National Park

Thursday, July 18, writing from Glacier National Park, Montana

We drove through North Dakota, crossed the border into Montana and headed for the town of Livingston. Our plans now are to visit Glacier National Park. Livingston used to be the home of Calamity Jane, and she lived there until she was arrested for disorderly conduct. A picture of her appears in one of their tour books. From her looks, it is easy to see why they called her *Calamity*.

Glacier National Park

As we approached Billings, Montana, we came upon an interstate exit with a sign announcing that we were approaching Pompy's Tower, and being curious, we turned off the interstate. Pompy's tower sits adjacent to the Yellowstone River and is a huge flat-topped rock poking out of the surrounding prairie to a height of 127 feet. On July 25, 1806, William Clark of Lewis & Clark fame, with nine men in his party, visited and climbed this rock. One of the men in Clark's party was a Frenchman named Toussant Charbonneau. Toussant brought his son on this historic journey, who was nicknamed Pomp by his fellow travelers. In contrast to Pomp, William Clark named the rock Pompy's Tower.

Before leaving the area, William Clark chiseled his name into the flanks of the tower for posterity and added these words to his journal: "*The Indians have made 2 piles of Stone on the top of this tower. The natives have engraved on the face of this rock the figures of animals &c. near which I marked my name and the day of the month & year*". I took a picture of Clark's inscription, but later, I accidentally erased it from my camera. This was the most memorable photograph I took on this journey, and now, for me, the historic inscription is only a memory. Someday, I will return to Pompy's tower and retake that photograph.

Like Mr. Clark, I climbed to the top of Pompy's tower and looked out upon a vista little changed from when he stood there almost two hundred years ago. But things have changed! When Meriwether Lewis and William Clark were commissioned by Thomas Jefferson to make their journey, very few Americans lived west of the Mississippi River. The population of the United States, at the time, was a little over 5 million people. Today, New York City's population is over 10 million people, and the population of the entire nation exceeds 326 million people. This is an increase of an astounding six thousand four hundred twenty percent (6,420%) in two hundred times. I wonder if 326 million people are sufficient for this nation, or should we allow these numbers to continue to grow so that the quality of our lives will increase accordingly? By the way, the world's population presently stands at 7.7 billion people. When William Clark carved his name into Pompey's Tower, there were 1.0 billion people in the world.

Pompy's Tower, near Billings, Montana, where William Clark of Lewis and Clark fame chiseled his name into the rock almost 200 years ago.
View of the Yellowstone River from the top of

Pompy's tower. Other than the road and field, this is what William Clark saw when he stood on this spot in 1806.

Upon passing Billings, Montana, we noticed a bluish haze on the horizon. As we drove closer, the haze began to look like clouds over a mountain range. Driving on, we realized that what we thought were clouds were really snow on the tops of the mountains. Lord, how I love this country, from a hundred and ten degrees in the shade to snow-capped mountains in a three-hour drive.

Scenery-wise, the Livingston area is magnificent. We are camped ten miles south of town, about fifty miles north of Yellowstone National Park. On both sides of us, mountains reach the sky. Grasslands extend up the sides of the mountains and end where the evergreen forests begin. Several homes are built at this transition point. I'll bet the view from their living rooms is spectacular.

A mountain view close to our campground in Livingston, Montana.

Montana is the fourth largest state in the Union, only exceeded in land area by Alaska, Texas, and California. Montana's name is derived from the Spanish word meaning "mountainous," and the western part of the state lives up to this description. The mountainous regions are famous for deposits of copper, gold, and silver and because of this bounty, the state is also known as "The Treasure State". On the other hand, the eastern side of the state is endless prairie that reaches as far as the eye can see. These spectacular and unspoiled vistas gave rise to the state also being called "The Big Sky Country". These open plains are home to vast herds of cattle, endless wheat fields, oil wells, and coal mines. Montana is truly a giant land of great contrasts. It is also the state where General George Armstrong Custer made his last stand and where the Nez Perce Indians fought their final battles against the United States Calvary.

This morning I drove into Livingston by motorcycle to buy provisions. As I write, I am sitting on a picnic table at our campsite, typing with my laptop on battery power. Earlier, I attempted to go online using our cell phone and did so successfully. I caught up on email and tried to send some pictures. The speed of my connection made this impossible, so I will have to forgo sending pictures until we find a campground with a phone line.

This afternoon, Gayle and I toured the area by motorcycle. We explored dirt roads on both sides of the valley until they dead-ended on the mountain slopes. The bike performed well, but with two people aboard, I had to be careful not to bite off more than I could chew. I did not want to chance a spill with Gayle on board. The scenery was spectacular and we took a lot of pictures. However, seeing the real thing takes your breath away and this can never be captured on film. Oops, I mean by electrons, as is the case with our digital camera.

After leaving Livingston, the road we were on ran through the center of a wide valley, fifteen to twenty miles across. We drove one hundred seventy-five miles and stopped in the town of Deer Lodge, the second-oldest city in Montana. In the 1850s Deer Lodge was a trading and trapping center. The town got its name because of a forty-foot-high cone that formed over a thermal spring that gave off copious amounts of vapor. From a distance, the cone and vapor resembled a smoking Indian lodge. This feature along with all the deer that grazed nearby gave the town its name. In 1883, the Northern Pacific Railroad arrived in Deer Lodge and the town then became the end of the line for pioneers heading west.

Deer Lodge's main claim to fame is that it is the home of the old Montana Territorial prison built in 1871 by convict labor. The prison was closed in 1979 and is now a museum. We took a walking tour of the prison and became convinced that you didn't want to be a criminal in Montana when this prison was being used. To say the least, it wasn't a very nice place. Its interior and exterior walls were whitewashed concrete and stone. The cell blocks were cold and drafty in the winter and hot and stifling in the summer. The holding cells for those prisoners foolish enough to misbehave were the size of a household closet, had no windows and only a bucket for bodily needs.

After touring the prison, we stopped in a local bistro on Main Street and hobnobbed with the locals. A couple we talked to lived back in the hills and used a wood-burning stove as their sole source of heat. What hearty souls they were. They hand-cut and split the wood they burned during the winter, and lived as if the past were still here today. The only thing modern about them was the truck they drove the fact that they had electricity. We swapped stories and bought each other beers. All the beers we sampled were from local microbreweries, and to say that they were excellent is an understatement. After I get home from this trip, I intend to write the Department of Tourism and urge them to rechristen Montana *The Beer State*.

On Wednesday, we left Deer Lodge and headed for Glacier National Park. Our plan is to depart the interstate, visit the park for two or three days, and then head north through Canada to pick up the east access route to Alaska. There are two ways to get to Alaska by road: the east access route, which passes east to west through central Canada, and the west access route out of Seattle, which hugs the continent's west coast.

We arrived in Glacier National Park area yesterday. It is Thursday morning and weather permitting; today, I hope to see my first glacier up close and personal.

Saturday, July 20, writing from Libby, Montana

There aren't any glaciers in Glacier National Park! At least we didn't see any on our tour. Instead, we saw a lot of snow banks, but I am getting ahead of myself. Presently, we are in Libby, Montana. Montana is so big, it's difficult to get out of. In any case, we toured Glacier National Park by motorcycle and put sixty-five miles on the bike.

Libby, Montana

The park, officially, is no longer Glacier National Park. Instead and it is now the Waterton-Glacier International Peace Park; Waterton, British Columbia, is the Canadian side of the park. Why we need a "peace park" with Canada escapes me. I guess it's to ensure they do not declare war on us.

In the 1800s, the area where Glacier National Park is now was home to the Blackfeet, Salish, and Kootenai Indians. The Blackfeet lived on the vast prairies east of the Park's mountains, while the Salish and Kootenai Indians lived and hunted in its western valleys. However, on occasion, they would penetrate into Blackfeet territory to hunt buffalo. In 1806, the Lewis and Clark Expedition came within 50 miles of the Park. As the area around the Park became settled, all three tribes were forced onto reservations. These Native American people still live near the Glacier National Park today, and the Park is of great spiritual significance to them.

Upon turning onto the access road that takes you into the park, we encountered a group of buildings filled with the usual tourist stuff. We made a point of passing by, and a mile or two down the road, paid Uncle Sam a ten-dollar park entry fee. Like most Americans, I feel Uncle Sam gets enough of my money through income tax, but I have to admit, this was the best ten dollars I ever spent.

At the onset, the two-lane park road is wide and for twenty-five miles, follows the heavily wooded shores of Lake McDonald. The turquoise blue water of this lake is snow melt and the water is as crystal clear as drinking water. After passing Lake McDonald, we followed a raging river that feeds the lake and began a modest climb into the mountains. The scenery was beautiful and spectacular. We moved through a wooded valley with rocky snow-banked peaks rising above us on both sides. I thought about how wonderful it would be to climb one of those peaks. What a view there must be from the summit.

A waterfall on the snowmelt fed river flowing into Lake McDonald in Glacier National Park.

Gayle posing near our motorcycle on the way to Logan's Pass.

After about five miles, the road narrowed and we came upon a sign advising that RV's and trucks were prohibited from going further. This was a harbinger of things to come. A short time later, we saw another sign which said passing was prohibited and we would be climbing a six percent grade for the next twelve miles. This got my attention and I was delighted when the road we were on switched back and headed up the side of the mountain I had wished to climb earlier.

A mountain view taken from the switch back where we began our climb to Logan's Pass.

We continued to backtrack up the lofty heights until finally reaching Logan's Pass, the Continental Divide, at an elevation of seven-thousand feet. Logan is the guy who built the road we were on and at the time of its construction, it was considered an engineering marvel. Driving this road was stupefying. In places, it was barely wide enough for two cars to pass and many stretches had no guard rail to keep vehicles from driving over cliffs that dropped thousands of feet into the valley below.

The narrow and risky road to Logan's Pass with an unprotected drop-off clearly evident.

The view looking back on the road to Logan's Pass. The line seen on the right across the middle of the mountains is the road we drove on the way to the pass.

Logan's Pass lies on the saddle of two peaks that rise two thousand feet higher into the sky. Melting snow was everywhere, and although the temperature was sixty degrees, much of the snow would linger until the following winter. Being an adventurer and one who likes to occasionally step outside the box, I decided to get a picture of the road we traveled from a rocky outcrop five hundred feet above the pass. After making this arduous climb, I neglected to remove the lens cap from my camera and, as a result, didn't get any pictures. I guess this was payback for breaking the rules.

Logan's Pass at the Continental Divide.

Adding insult to injury, upon descending, I was accosted by a park ranger who politely reminded me that tourists were not supposed to leave the designated paths. Apparently, this rule is justified by the belief that if they allowed people to walk off the paths, then the whole place would look like a path. Being sympathetic to this concern, I apologized for almost ruining the park for all those who would follow and proceeded to find Gayle. Upon locating her, I was amused to learn that she was unaware of my climb, even though I could see her clearly on the way up.

Presently, Gayle and I are in Libby, Montana, camped in a secluded and wooded RV park. Our site is immediately adjacent to a gurgling brook, which lulled us into a restful sleep last night. We will spend time here cleaning our motor home and getting it ready for the Canadian part of our journey which begins forty miles up the road.

CHAPTER 3

The Road to Jasper

Monday, July 23, writing from just across the Canadian border

We spent three nights in Libby purging the road dust from our pores and getting the RV ready for the next leg of our journey. Until now, we felt we were traveling somewhere else, with Alaska being the ultimate goal. Now, Alaska is the only goal, or so we thought.

We drove back to Libby on US 2 and took a left onto Highway 37, a seventy-mile dog leg that passes Libby Dam on its way to Highway 93. We had seen some wonderful scenery in Glacier National Park, but the views on this road were also impressive. The road followed the Kootenay River. Twenty miles outside of Libby, we arrived at Libby Dam. It wasn't as big as Hoover, but still was a very big dam by anyone's reckoning. Lake Kootenay, formed by the dam, was also huge; a mile across and fifty miles long. It extended all the way to Roosville near the Canadian border. As we traveled, Gayle could not stop taking pictures.

A view of Lake Kootenay behind Libby Dam in Montana.

I made a fuss about the scenery in the Dakota Badlands, a bigger fuss about the sights in Glacier National Park, and lauded the scenery on Highway 37. This being the case, what is left to say about the Canadian Rockies in British Columbia? God, they are awesome. The highest point of land in South Florida is the Pompano Beach landfill, a monument to the doings of man. The higher points of land in British Columbia turn the Pompano landfill into a pimple and are monuments to the doings of God. As we traveled Route 93, still following the Kootenai River valley, the rocky peaks on both sides of us extended as far as the eye could see. We drove for hours mesmerized by the beauty around us and finally stopped in the town of Radium Junction. I have no idea how this place got its name, but when I looked at Gayle her nose was glowing.

A scenic view along Highway 93 on the way to Radium Junction, British Columbia.

A scenic view of the Kootenay River along Highway 93 on the way to Radium Junction, British Columbia.

At a rest stop in British Columbia, Gayle, myself, and Sally on the right with Scooter on the left.

British Columbia is Canada's third-largest province and is as big as the areas of California, Oregon, and Washington combined. More than half of British Columbia's residents live in the southwestern corner of the province, which has a relatively mild climate and fertile lowlands suitable for farming. British Columbia is known for its natural beauty, rugged coastlines, magnificent, forested mountains, pristine lakes and rivers, and abundant wildlife. Three-fifths of Canada's lumber comes from British Columbia, and its many mines produce significant quantities of coal, copper, gold, silver, zinc, and other minerals.

Tomorrow, we head for the town of Jasper. We will travel two hundred miles through three adjoining Canadian National Parks: Yoho, Banff, and Jasper. We were told that the scenery in these parks is breathtaking, and I am intrigued by one place on the map designated as "ice fields". I trust this means we will have free ice for our cooler. "The Milepost", an indispensable traveler's guide for anyone going to Alaska, says that Jasper National Park is home to moose, elk, bighorn sheep, and grizzlies; all of which may be seen from the comfort of our motor home while traveling.

An alpine glacier in Jasper National Park.

A snowmelt lake in Jasper National Park.

A mountain scene in Jasper National Park with mountains that seem to go on forever. This photo was taken through the windshield of our RV while driving. The smudges you see on the sky and clouds are bug spatter.

Wednesday, July 24, writing from Jasper National Park, Alberta, Canada

We are presently camped in Jasper, and I am at a loss for words to describe the natural beauty of the three parks we drove through. The views, the scenery, the mountains, the valleys, the rivers, the forests, all were beyond description, and words could never do justice in describing these truly wondrous works of nature.

We left Radium Junction around nine-thirty this morning. About five miles into Yoho, the first of the three parks, we rounded a bend and a cow moose blocked the road. Several miles later, we watched a coyote scurry across the highway. I used second gear a lot during the day, both up and down hills. We never saw any grizz. However, the mountain goats were plentiful, and we visited three glaciers along the way. This place must be a real icebox in the winter. I wonder how the animals survive.

We pulled into a campground for the night, and for the first time in our journey will be "boondocking". This expression is commonly used to describe camping without the benefit of external hookups, as is done in remote areas. However, I prefer the expression "free camping" because camping in this manner is free of hookups and usually doesn't cost anything. Furthermore, you can free camp anywhere, in wilderness areas or Wal-Mart parking lots. I find it a stretch to think of camping at Wal-Mart as being in the boondocks.

Our motor home is well-equipped for free camping. It has propane for heating, cooking, and refrigeration, holding tanks for storing sewage and wastewater, and a generator and batteries that provide electric power. My generator is gas-powered and big enough to run all the motor home's electrical appliances, even with both air-conditioners turned on. Most national parks provide camping for RVs, but only in designated areas, and there usually is a fee for doing so, even if water and electricity are not available. The onboard generator can always be used to provide power, but its hours of operation are usually limited because of how noisy it is when running. This is of real concern when tent campers are nearby. Jasper was no exception to these rules.

How perceptions change as you get older. For most of my life, I have been a tent camper and looked down upon those "softies" sitting in their big rigs watching television. From my perspective, they were nincompoops. If all they came here to do was watch television, why don't they camp in their driveways at home and leave the wilderness to people who appreciate Mother Nature? I guess the reality of my situation is that now I am the nincompoop. However, while my sympathies are still with the tent campers, for some reason, I find it hard to feel guilty as I sit here sipping a gin tonic as Gayle prepares a couple of "T" bones for the grill.

Upon waking this morning, I took the dogs for a walk and encountered three female elk in a field near the road. I wondered how close I could get before they spooked. As I approached, four more females appeared out of the woods. Despite my two yapping dogs, they held their ground. I approached within a hundred feet and decided to back off. A deer is a deer, but these girls were a lot bigger than the deer I'm used to seeing, and there were seven of them. It was survival of the smartest. If they are not afraid of me and my dogs, then maybe I should be afraid of them?

Upon returning to the RV, I told Gayle about my encounter with the elk. A short time later, much to our delight, one of these woodland beasts came walking down the road nibbling foliage as she went. As this elk passed us, she sniffed our rearview mirror and proceeded to meander down the road. I got my camera, exited the RV, and followed her from about twenty feet away. Wild animals in Jasper National Park; hogwash! I now believe that some of them are trained and put back in the wild to attract and entertain tourists. What a con! I'm surprised there are no roadside quarter-operated gumball machines so people can buy food to feed them.

Our campground visitor in Jasper National Park.

We left Jasper and turned onto Canadian Highway 16. Mountains and beautiful scenery everywhere, ho-hum! We were now following the Fraser River valley, heading toward the city of Prince George. As we traveled, the mountains started shrinking. The farther we drove, the smaller they became until we were driving through forested rolling hills. Not being in a national park anymore, other tourists were gone, and most of the time, there was no one else on the road. Ten or so minutes would go by without seeing another vehicle, and this gave us an appreciated respite to soak in the beautiful scenery as we drove. All my life, I have felt there were too many people in the world, but now I know there are places left where you can be free of them. I find a measure of solace in this.

A view of the Fraser River off of Canadian Highway 16 on the way to Prince George.

And speaking of people getting away from people, I have to say something about the bikers, not bikers as in motorcycles, but bikers as in *on a bicycle*. As we drove, we encountered men and women peddling their way through the back country, packing tents and gear for wilderness camping. Talk about being upstaged as a mindless buffoon in a monster RV. I respect these rugged souls. They have the courage and fortitude to experience Mother Nature in a very close and personal way. I am sure they see a lot more wildlife than we do, and not just animals trained to attract tourists.

Upon reaching Prince George, which is a city of seventy-five thousand people centrally located in British Columbia, we stopped at a supermarket to resupply and then headed north on Canadian Route 97. The supermarket was unique because most everything being sold was in bulk and offered from barrels. From coffee to pie fillings, it was all there in bulk. We were delighted as we inspected the six or seven aisles of barreled foodstuffs.

After leaving Prince George, we drove about fifty more miles and camped in a small Provincial Park on McLeod Lake. As I type, I am about thirty feet from the water. The tranquility of the moment makes my mind wander to my friends back home. I surmise that, as I write, they are driving home from work and stuck in a traffic jam. Some people have it tough, but fortunately, none of them are around here.

CHAPTER 4

On the Road in British Columbia

Thursday, July 25, writing from Sikanni River, British Columbia

We left McLeod Lake at about nine-thirty this morning and planned to fuel up in Chetwynd, about one hundred miles to the north. As we drove, the mountains increased in size but were nothing like those in Jasper. The scenery was beautiful. We gassed and had lunch in Chetwynd and asked a local if Route 29, a cutoff that bypassed Dawson Creek, was a good road. He said it was and added that it was the most scenic route. Accepting this at face value, we turned onto Route 29 and drove along the Peace River, enjoying the sights. Soon, we noticed a road, several miles in the distance, climbing the side of a mountain. I jokingly said to Gayle that the road up ahead was the one we were on. She blurted out, "You've got to be kidding me!"

I repeated this joke every time our road turned toward the offending grade. However, it soon became apparent that the joke was on me. As we approached this roadway to the clouds, I slowed to thirty, put the RV in second gear, and started climbing at 3500 RPM. The motor screamed as we sharply switched up the mountain. When we finally made it to the top, I exhaled a sigh of relief. However, we soon came upon a sign reading "10% Downhill Grade Ahead". Slowing again and downshifting, we braked and switched back down the backside of the mountain we had just climbed. We repeated this frightening ride one more time before reaching the end of Route 29. I am not sure if my motor and transmission are supposed to handle this kind of abuse, but even if they can, I intend to take Route 97 and go through Dawson Creek on the way home.

Dawson Creek is the start of the Alaska Highway. The road used to be called the Alcan Highway, a contraction of Alaskan/Canadian Highway. I have no idea why they changed the name, especially in consideration of the fact that dropping the name's Canadian half is politically incorrect. In any case, the Alaska Highway begins in Dawson Creek, is about one thousand four hundred miles long, and ends in Delta Junction, Alaska, about one hundred miles shy of Fairbanks.

Construction on the Alaska Highway began in 1942, and the road was completed in twenty months by the Army Corps of Engineers. The purpose of the road was to facilitate the support of military bases in Alaska. The bases were there to counter the Japanese threat to the United States through the Aleutian Island chain. The Japanese made one attempt to invade and set up a beachhead on the lower end of the Aleutians. Fortunately, their incursion was ill-fated and short-lived. Immediately following the war, traveling the Alaska Highway was a risky adventure, but through the years, the road has been improved such that the risks are now minimal during the summer.

Upon reaching the end of what should be described as the "infamous" Route 29 cutoff, we finally turned onto the Alaska Highway (Route 97). To our surprise, at this juncture, it was a four-lane divided highway, good-shouldered and well-maintained. The scenery was similar to the farmlands of Pennsylvania. As we drove, the farms disappeared, and we soon found ourselves driving through rolling hills covered by densely packed pine forests. The scenery was beautiful. As the distant mountains drew closer, we decided to stop for the night at the Sikanni River RV Park, nine hundred seventy-five miles from the Alaskan Border.

A view of the Sikanni River RV Park. Our RV is on the far left. The bridge to the right is the Alaska Highway.

The Sikanni River is a swiftly moving stream about seventy feet across. At the park office, I met a dumb Indian. Not dumb as in *dumb as a box of rocks*, but dumb because he had lost his ability to speak. He was a friendly sort and struck up a conversation with me using sign language. He explained that he had caught two trout this morning and had them for lunch. I also learned that he used to ride in a rodeo and quit because his horse threw him against a post, breaking his leg and foot in several places. Meeting this Indian was a rewarding and enjoyable experience. Despite his handicap, he was warm, friendly, and all smiles as he spoke with his hands. What a life this man has led. I'll bet he has never been stuck in a traffic jam and probably doesn't even know what one is.

A picture of Scooter and Sally in our RV, waiting for me to come inside and feed them. They always wait for me to come inside and feed them.

Friday, July 26, writing from somewhere about 50 miles North of Fort Nelson, British Columbia

This morning, after cleaning several pounds of mashed bugs off the front of our motor home, I belatedly installed the wire mesh screen I had prepared in Pennsylvania to protect my radiator and transmission cooler. Sufficient quantities of bugs will clog this equipment and may result in an overheat condition and possible equipment failure. We left Sikanni River around noon anticipating more mountains ahead. To our surprise the terrain flattened and this leg of journey was smooth and uneventful.

The main roads in these parts are different from those we are familiar with back home. They are well-maintained with two opposing lanes of traffic, but here is where the similarity ends. Their shoulders are relatively narrow and they have severe drop-offs on both sides of the road. Despite this, there are no guard rails to keep a wayward car or truck from, literally, falling off the road.

I surmise that the drop-offs are there to allow huge quantities snow to be plowed off the road during the winter and guard rails would hinder this process. This being the case, if you are unfortunate and drive off the road's shoulder, you probably will a need crane to get your car back on the road. Such was the case with a truck we saw several miles back. They were still working to put out the fire caused by the accident as we passed.

We drove one hundred sixty-three miles today, and the forests along the way were awesome. Another characteristic of northern roads is that, in most places, the forest is cleared back about one hundred yards or so from the road's edge. This adds considerably to the view, but I think that the real reason this is done is to allow drivers to see wildlife approaching the road and thereby avoid a collision. Back east, when a car hits a deer, the deer lies dead on the side of the road, and the damaged vehicle drives off. Up here, when a car hits a moose, it is totaled, and the moose walks off.

We were not disappointed with today's drive. After being warned by road signs that moose were in the area, we finally spotted a cow and her calf about a half mile ahead. I slowed to take pictures. However, the moose had other ideas, and when we were about fifty yards away, both she and her calf bolted across the road, necessitating hard braking on my part. You can't imagine how huge these animals are. The cow was as high as my windshield and had to be at least nine hundred pounds. Males can weigh in at twice that much.

An encounter with a moose and her calf on the Alaska Highway.

I cannot tell you exactly where we are camped right now because, for the first time, we are truly "free camping". We pulled off the road just past Fort Nelson, British Columbian, found a level spot, and set up for the night. I am typing on generator power while Gayle prepares steaks for the grill. She prepares; I cook! We have everything we could possibly need, hot and cold water, a shower, a stove, a grill, a television, a refrigerator, heat, and a comfortable queen-size bed. The only thing missing is other people, and for some unexplainable reason, I can't bring myself to miss them.

Saturday, July 27, writing from the Liard River Bridge about 75 miles south of the Yukon border

Yesterday, after traveling one hundred fifty-eight miles in four hours, we stopped for lunch at a turnoff near the Liard River Bridge. The area was so picturesque, we decided to free-camp there for the night, but I am getting ahead of myself. Upon leaving our campsite this morning, the beautiful road we were on turned into what one would expect from the Alaska Highway: narrow, with almost non-existent shoulders and winding through mountainous terrain. In most places, our speed was limited to thirty miles per hour, and for most of the drive, we felt like we were on a roller coaster. Foolishly, I did not study the map before leaving this morning and had no idea we would be negotiating Summit Lake Pass, in Stone Mountain Provincial Park, followed shortly by Muncho Pass, in Muncho Lake Provincial Park.

The stretch of Alaska Highway that traverses Muncho Lake Provincial Park is fifty-five miles long, and it is said that this drive is the most scenic on the Alaska Highway. Copper oxide deposits leaching from bedrock have colored the waters of Muncho a deep blue color and this is in sharp contrast to the light grey vertical cliffs that surround the lake. Mountain goats frolicked on the sides of these cliffs as if they were playing in a grassy field. It was an amazing sight to see. How these animals could be so at home on such treacherous terrain is mind-boggling. We also saw numerous mountain goat, caribou, and Dall's sheep as we traveled through both of these parks. Needless to say, the scenery took our breath away and this was a very exciting segment of our journey.

Mountain goats on the road to Muncho Lake Provincial Park.

Mountain goats frolicking on the cliffs near Muncho Lake.

Prior to stopping for the night, the road improved, but we had no idea how long it would stay that way. According to the map, the next two hundred miles should be mountain-free, so I expect we will have an easier drive.

CHAPTER 5

The Yukon

Sunday, July 28, writing from Teslin, Yukon Province, Canada

The road to Teslin was better than expected, but still offered some surprises. There was a twenty-mile stretch through a mountain pass that was just as bad as the road we were on yesterday. We also drove through three miles of heavy construction, followed by nine miles of improved dirt road. According to a group of our fellow travelers, this will be the last stretch of dirt road we will encounter on the Alaska Highway. I hope they are right. The road was excellent for the last ninety miles, and we were able to cruise at seventy miles per hour in places.

As we traveled, we decided to make a game of counting the vehicles we saw for the next hundred miles on our odometer. We counted ninety-one vehicles, eighty-four heading the opposite direction, and seven traveling our way. During the entire day's travel, a distance of two hundred sixty-seven miles, we passed a total of six people touring on bicycles. In consideration of how remote the roads were on this leg of our journey, I was surprised by this number.

About ten minutes into the start of the day's journey, we came upon a male buffalo grazing on the side of the road. We were thrilled to see such a magnificent creature so close to the road. However, a short time later, imagine our excitement when we encountered a herd of about fifty individuals scattered on both sides of the highway. We stopped in the middle of the herd, and I took pictures from the steps of our RV. The buffalo did not seem to mind us being there, but I didn't want to risk provoking them by getting closer.

Three members of the buffalo herd we encountered on our way to the Yukon Territory.

Later that morning, we crossed into the Yukon and stopped in the Town of Watson Lake. In 1895, the Yukon was made a district of the North West Territories and three years later it became a separate territory. Robert Campbell, a British fur trader working for the Hudson's Bay Company, was the first non-Indian to explore the Yukon. In 1848, he established a trading post on the Pelly River at Fort Selkirk. The Yukon is home to about 32,000 people about 6,000 of them being Indians from the Tlingit and Gwich'in tribes. Each year over 400,000 visitors traverse the Yukon heading for Alaska on the Alaska Highway. The primary tourist attraction in the Yukon is Dawson City, which is near the site of the gold strike that resulted in the great gold rush of "98". Downtown Dawson has changed little since the gold rush days and many original buildings are still standing and in use.

At the border between British Columbia and the Yukon Territory. At least they don't waste a lot of money on signs around here.

Watson Lake is home of the Signpost Forrest. The forest was started in 1942, by a soldier working on the construction of the Alaska Highway. He put up the first signs showing the mileage to New York, Chicago, Edmonton and Whitehorse. Other workers, nostalgic for home, added their signs. Following their example, tourists now add signs from all over the world. At present, there are approximately eighty thousand signs in the forest and there is no end in sight to their number.

Watson Lake is the first town you come to as you enter the Yukon, and because of this, the town prides itself on being the *Gateway to the Yukon*. The town was named after Frank Watson, a Californian who came to the area in search of gold in the spring of 1898. Frank, who was able to earn a decent living working his placer claim, married an Indian girl and never left the area.

Frank and his Indian wife settled into a cabin on the shores of the lake, which now also bears his name. Today, Watson Lake is an important transportation and distribution hub for mining and logging activities in southern Yukon, northern British Columbia.

The Watson Lake sign forest in British Columbia.

As we drove out of Watson Lake, we encountered miles of stone graffiti on both sides of the road. People have written their names and other messages on the sloping roadside shoulders by placing round stones of varying size, end to end, to form letters. It is a sight to see! Some of these messages must have taken days to construct because they are quite elaborate. I was tempted to stop and add our names to this impromptu tourist attraction. However, we had to move on, and I knew I would not be happy contributing something that did not rival the more elaborate presentations.

A view from the Alaska Highway between Watson Lake and Whitehorse with fireweed in the foreground.

Presently, we are stopped for the night in the town of Teslin, a town of two hundred souls, most of whom are Indians. Teslin, a town on a lake with the same name, is an active tourist stop for those traveling the Alaska Highway. Prior to the construction of the Alaska Highway in 1922, Teslin was only a trading post for Indians dealing furs trapped in the area. Once the Highway was constructed, Teslin became a permanent settlement, and tourism became its primary industry. We had our first taste of Halibut this evening in a nearby restaurant. It was excellent. Tonight, sunset will occur at approximately eleven o'clock, and the sun will set even later the farther north we travel. Tomorrow we will stop in Whitehorse, the Capital of the Yukon, and a city of thirty-two thousand people.

We spent the day sightseeing in the city of Whitehorse. The town was named after the nearby Yukon River rapids by *Stampeders* from the gold rush of 1898. The rapidly flowing white water resembled the flowing manes of galloping white horses; thus, the town's name. The rapids are gone and were displaced by a lake that formed when the Whitehorse Dam was constructed. Whitehorse's claims to fame are the staging rolls it played in gold rush of 1898 and construction of the Alaska Highway in 1942.

While in Whitehorse, we visited the Transportation Museum, the Beringia Centre, and the Whitehorse Dam salmon fish ladder. The fish ladder is a series of water-filled steps that permit migrating salmon to bypass the dam. During the summer months, you are able to observe the salmon negotiate these steps through windows provided for this purpose in an adjoining building. The Beringia Centre is a museum of the Ice Age past of the area, focusing on the wildlife that lived on the land bridge which connected Alaska to Russia. The Bering Strait presently covers this pathway to Asia. One exhibit was a life-size reproduction of a woolly mammoth. As I looked at this magnificent beast, my mouth began to water. I couldn't help thinking of all the mammoth burgers he would make. It was an interesting and enjoyable day.

A picture of a mail and passenger sled, in the Whitehorse Transportation Museum, that was used to travel to Whitehorse at the turn of the century.

The Whitehorse Dam salmon fish ladder.

We are now only about 300 miles from Alaska and plan to spend one more day free camping before we get there.

Wednesday, July 31, writing from the Alaskan Hwy, 3.2 miles past the Donjek River Bridge, Population 0

Convinced that we were finally through the dirt and dust, we washed the RV before we left our campground in Whitehorse. The road we encountered went from being the best to the worst of our journey; the worst being three construction areas, several miles in length, where the going was twenty to twenty-five miles per hour. A lot of good washing the RV did! As we traveled, snow-capped mountains loomed in the distance. We drove by Kluane Lake, a forty-mile-long body of clear sky-blue water. What a sight to see!

A view of the Alaska Highway north of Whitehorse

Another scene from the Alaska Highway north of Whitehorse.

I began to notice sections of abandoned road adjacent to one we were on. I surmised they were older sections of that Alaska Highway that were cut off when the improved road was built. Our plan was to stop and free camp after our odometer turned 200 miles. This happened directly upon the Donjek River Bridge. Three miles down the road we spotted a spur heading into the woods. Turning onto the spur, we saw that it ran for several hundred yards into the bush and ended in a "T". The "T" was formed by a gravel parking area that extended a few hundred feet in both directions. On the left was a fast-running stream, so we backed into the higher ground on the right and set up camp. No one could see us from the road where we were parked and this provided us with privacy and a sense of security.

Free camped on a cut-off spur of the original Alaska Highway near the Donjek River.

Gazing up and down the graveled parking area, narrow grassy fields extended into the distance in both directions. It occurred to me that the only explanation for what I saw is that we are presently camped on a section of the original Alaska Highway that was cut off when the road was improved. The area where we are parked, in all probability, was used as a staging area for vehicles working on the newer section of road. Later, this theory proved correct when I took the dogs for a walk. Several hundred yards from where we were parked, I came upon a twisted and rusty automobile bumper. A short distance later, I rounded a bend and was delighted to see a still-standing highway "S" curve warning sign. I stared at this sign and wondered what tales it would tell if it could only talk.

Picture 25 –
A cut-off section of the original Alaska Highway near the Donjek River.

What a beautiful spot we have found. We have our own private campground, ringed by snowcapped mountains, with a gurgling brook nearby to lull us into a state of serene contentment. The nearer mountains are covered with brush and grass. The closest one rises approximately one thousand five hundred feet above where we are parked. As I gazed at its craggy summit, I noticed white specks here and there which, at first, I thought were small patches of snow. Curious, I broke my binoculars and was delighted to discover that the white patches were Dall's sheep grazing on the lofty peaks. Dall's sheep are a smaller version of the Bighorn Sheep. I counted twenty individuals in one herd. What a thrilling sight they were!

A mountain view from our "free" campground near the Alaska border. The white specks seen on the top of the mountain are Dall's sheep.

We bedded down at eleven o'clock last night and it was still light out. I have no idea when the sun set, but the temperature started to drop rapidly once the sun went behind the mountains. The daytime high was sixty degrees. However, the air is so dry and the sun so bright that it feels a lot warmer than that. I took my walk yesterday wearing only jeans and a T-shirt. Upon waking up this morning the thermometer was pegged at thirty degrees.

Today will be a banner day in our journey and in my life. The Alaskan border is only 80 miles away and crossing it will be the fulfillment of my lifelong dream.

CHAPTER 6

Tok to Fairbanks

Friday, August 2, Writing from Tok, Alaska, Population 1,500

Secretary of State William Seward bought Alaska from Russia in 1867 for a little over seven million dollars, or about two cents per acre. At the time, the purchase was derided as being Seward's Folly, Seward's Icebox, and Icebergia. However, most Americans supported the acquisition, and as things turned out, Alaska's natural resources have repaid Americans the price of this purchase many times over. Alaska is the largest state in the union and is one-fifth as big as all the other states combined. However, it ranks forty-seventh in population. Mainland Alaska is only 51 miles from Russia, and it was the Russians who first explored the state and exploited its resources.

A picture of me standing at the Canadian/Alaskan border.

The Alaska Range is taken from just across the border on our way to Tok.

Tok. Alaska (pronounced *toke* as if you were taking one) is a town of one thousand five hundred people that prides itself on being the *Gateway to Alaska*. It is ninety-six miles from the Canadian border on the intersection of Glenn Highway (Route #1) and the Alaska Highway (Route #2). The Glenn Highway heads southwest, three hundred twenty-six miles, to Anchorage, and the Alaska Highway heads northwest and ends in Delta Junction about one hundred miles away. However, Route #1 continues on through Delta Junction as the Taylor Highway, for another one hundred miles, terminating in Fairbanks. Completing this large triangle and connecting Fairbanks to Anchorage, a distance of three-hundred sixty-two miles, is the George Parks Highway (Route #3).

Our campground in Tok. Notice the fireweed in the foreground and our camper, just to the right of the center of the picture, sporting its newly installed bra.

At the Tok campground dump station on our way out. The bra didn't look like much, but it was effective and cheap. Notice that after its installation, I could no longer use my windshield wipers. An application of Rain X solved this problem for me.

After regrouping, our intentions are to travel this Alaskan triangle from Tok to Fairbanks, to Anchorage, and back to Tok. Ignoring side trips, the total distance we will travel is eight hundred ninety-eight miles. It will take approximately thirty days to make this circuit, and the order of business along the way will be sightseeing, gold panning, fishing, exploring, and hunting for a mammoth frozen in a glacier. We would like to be out of Alaska by the end of August to avoid a possible early winter snowstorm. On the road to Tok, we passed several road signs that said chains were permitted after September 15th. I assume that if they are permitted after that date, it is because they may be needed.

Sunday, August 4, writing from Delta Junction, Alaska, Population 3,000

Tok is a town that exists primarily because of tourists, and it is the focal point of everyone visiting Alaska by road. At four in the afternoon, the main drag turns into an RV traffic jam with rigs rolling in from Canada and other areas around the state.

We bought gas at the town's Texaco gas station and also found and bought a gold panning kit in the station's convenience store. The kit included a plastic gold pan, a magnifying glass, a plastic eyedropper, a magnet, instructions, and a bag of gold-bearing dirt. The purpose of the pan is obvious; it is used for panning for gold. The magnifying glass is for examining the gold you find. I find the inclusion of this particular piece of equipment to be discouraging. How rich can you get from gold that you need a magnifying glass to see? The magnet is for distinguishing real gold from magnetite, which is also known as iron pyrite; the infamous "fool's gold". The eyedropper is for sucking up tiny gold flakes out of your pan. Finally, the bag of gold-bearing dirt is used to practice panning for gold. We found nine tiny gold flakes in our bag. Whoopee! When I say tiny, I am talking about specks far smaller than the head of a match.

After our success with the gold-bearing dirt, we were ready to put our newly developed skill to the test in the field. We tried two streams on the way to Delta Junction, and the only thing we found was fool's gold. You have to be a fool to be fooled by fool's gold because there are many differences between the two substances. Fool's gold is magnetic, while real gold is not. Gold is found at the bottom of your pan. Pyrite rests on top of the silt and sand. Gold, a soft metal, flattens when hit. Pyrite, being a mineral, shatters. Gold has a dull luster to it. Pyrite glitters and shines. However, the most telling test is that pyrite is easily found, while gold is not.

Thirty miles short of Delta Junction, we came upon the Black Veterans Memorial Bridge. It used to be called the Gerstle River Bridge. The Gerstle River was named after Mr. Lewis Gerstle, president of the Alaska Commercial Company, who provided support to Army Lt. Henry Allen when he mapped and explored the Copper, Tanana, and Koyukuk rivers at the request of the War Department in 1885. The Gerstle River, also mapped and explored by Lt. Allen, had no name at the time, so he honored Mr. Gerstle by naming the river after him.

The Gerstle River, taken from the Black Veterans Memorial Bridge. It was now August, so the river had been reduced to a group of meandering rivulets. In the spring, snowmelt will turn this pastoral river into a raging torrent with the water up to the tree line on both sides of the river.

In 1993, a bill sponsored by Alaskan Congressional Representative Bettye Davis from Anchorage, renamed the bridge the Black Veterans Memorial Bridge to honor the 3,695 black soldiers of the 93rd, 94th, 97th, and 388th Engineering General Service Regiments who worked on the Alcan Highway as it was known then. A total of 10,607 soldiers from these regiments worked on the highway; thus, one out of three of them were black and Representative Davis as well as the rest of Congress, wanted to commemorate this special effort by Black Americans.

Delta Junction, the terminus of the Alaska Highway, is little over one hundred miles from Tok and about halfway to Fairbanks. The road between Delta Junction and Tok was in good shape compared to the drive from Whitehorse to Alaska. During that earlier stretch, we received a bad ding in our windshield from a rock tossed up by a passing car doing seventy miles per hour in a graveled work zone marked thirty-five. Locals care very little about nincompoops driving around in their ostentatious RV's. As a result of this minor tragedy, I belatedly installed the vinyl bra I made back in Pennsylvania. A bra is a vinyl boot that covers the front of the RV with the exception of its windshield and headlights. Mine extends partway up the bottom of the windshield and would have saved us from the hit we endured.

This evening, we drove into town for a few drinks in a local bar. We met Barcardi Bob and Pepe. Barcardi Bob, about my age, hails from Minnesota and moved to Alaska when he was 16. Pepe was from Mexico. He visited Alaska 17 years ago and hasn't gotten around to leaving yet. According to our newly found friends, the primary activities in Delta Junction are fishing and drinking. They also told us that there isn't much gold in the area, so we will hold off panning again until we get to Fairbanks. Fairbanks is a gold-rich area and owes its existence to a nearby gold strike.

Monday, August 5, writing from Fairbanks, Alaska, Population 82,440

We left Delta Junction late this morning and drove one hundred miles to Fairbanks through the smoke from several forest fires. We could not see the fires themselves, so they were not close enough to be of concern. However, they were near enough to create a fog-like haze that degraded the view of some very impressive scenery. We also saw several moose grazing alongside the road.

A moose feeding alongside the road between Delta Junction and Fairbanks.

Leaving Delta Junction, we also got our first look at a section of the Alaska Pipeline. The pipeline is one of the longest in the world and stretches eight hundred miles from Prudhoe Bay on Alaska's North Slope to Valdez, Alaska, its terminus. The pipeline was completed in 1977 and cost 8 billion dollars to build. It is forty-eight inches in diameter and delivers twenty-five percent of the Nation's oil to the lower forty-eight. During its journey, the pipeline crosses three mountain ranges and eight hundred rivers and streams.

The Alaska Pipeline at one of its many river crossings. The picture is hazy, not because of mist, but because of wildfires burning throughout the state.

The road to Fairbanks was level, in good condition, and traveled through wilderness for its first forty miles. As we got closer to Fairbanks, more and more roadside homes began to appear. Tanana Lake, about 50 miles from Fairbanks, was dotted with vacation homes owned by the city's residents.

Fairbanks is anything but a frontier wilderness town. Instead, it is a metropolitan area with all of the important amenities of life: Wal-Mart, Home Depot, McDonald's, Pizza Hut, Wendy's, Subway, etc., the full catastrophe. We have driven over five thousand miles from Florida to see a place that, from a merchandising point of view, is no different from Fort Lauderdale.

Thursday, August 8, writing from Fairbanks, Alaska

We spent the last two days in Fairbanks shopping, relaxing, and reading. Yesterday morning, upon getting up, the smoke was gone because the wind had changed direction and the sun was shining brightly. After breakfast, I unloaded the bike and drove around town to pick up supplies. There is nothing we have in the lower forty-eight that can't be found in Fairbanks, but the real find of my shopping spree was a book entitled, *Where to Prospect for Gold in Alaska Without Getting Shot*, by Ron Wendt. With this book, my dream of striking it rich was about to come true.

In the afternoon, Gayle and I visited American Legion Post #11, and were greeted as if we were old friends. Don, whom we met at the bar, was a forty-year resident of Alaska. He must have dropped over a hundred dollars playing bar games as we talked about gold and how to find it. Our conversation tempered my enthusiasm somewhat.

Gold panning is a *separating process* that works because gold is heavier than dirt. As you swirl a mixture of dirt and water around, the gold sinks to the bottom of the pan and is caught in its grooves. The water and dirt are then poured over the lip of the pan, leaving the gold behind. This same separating action also takes place in the streams where gold is found. Therefore, to find sufficient quantities of gold, you do not find a likely place, scoop up a pan full of dirt, and strike it rich. Initially, you may find a flake or two, but after doing so, the work really begins.

If there is gold in a particular stream in significant quantities, it lies beneath the mud and gravel close to bedrock. Gravity and the agitating action of the water ensure this is the case. Therefore, if you want to strike it rich, in addition to a pan, you will also need a pick and a shovel. Once so equipped and once you have found the right spot, all that needs to be done, provided you have filed a claim, is dig through tons of gravel and mud while standing in the water of an ice-cold stream. To say the least, this is not easy and not fun.

There is one bright spot in this gloomy picture. We have a metal detector which will find missed nuggets anywhere dredging has previously occurred. This includes the shoulders of highways, which sometimes are made up of the tailings from gold dredging operations. According to our instruction book, using a metal detector for the first time in her life, a woman found a sixteen-ounce gold nugget on the shoulder of Elliott Highway, just north of Fairbanks. This is the good news. The bad news is that several months later, they found her frozen to death on the side of the road with her nugget clutched in one hand and her metal detector clutched in the other. For the first time in our journey, I am glad that Gayle is terrified of driving the motor home. She will be the one who will hang off our rear bumper, holding the metal detector over the road's shoulder as we drive.

I always thought of Alaska as being a pristine paradise, and it is in most places. However, as I write, there are fifty-seven wildfires burning throughout the State, and according to the evening news, the state is not immune to kidnapping and the murdering of children. This morning's heavy rain should dampen some of the forest fires. Unfortunately, it will do nothing to help the unfortunate children we just heard about on the news.

I guess it's true that people are people no matter where you go, and some of them aren't worth a plugged nickel, even in paradise. The litter we found evident at several rest stops also bears testimony to this. Can you imagine living here or visiting Alaska because of its awesome beauty and then littering the roads and rest stops, marrying that beauty for all who follow? And to do this when roadside trash containers are available everywhere? The longer I live, the more ashamed I am of my own species.

Today, we head north from Fairbanks to the gold fields on the Steese Highway.

CHAPTER 7

The White Mountains Adventure

Friday, August 9, writing from a tailings site, 5 miles Northeast of Fox, Population 320

We headed north out of Fairbanks and drove about ten miles to Fox. Fox, Alaska, with a population of 300 people, is not much more than a gas station and a few stores on the intersections of Route #2 out of Fairbanks and the Steese Highway (Route #6). For most of the way, the short drive up was on a modern four-lane divided highway, but the fog and smoke made traveling surreal and eerie. Just shy of Fox, we came upon Gold Dredge #8 and decided to visit this historic relic. The tour was interesting and informative. Afterward, we continued to Fox and, upon arriving there, turned right onto the Steese Highway.

Gold Dredge #8, forever stranded on Route #2, just north of Fairbanks.

The digging blade and dredging buckets of Gold Dredge #8.

We are now heading for Nome Creek in the White Mountains National Recreation Area, sixty miles to the north. According to Ron Wendt, if we are lucky, our dreams of becoming rich will soon be realized. About fifteen miles out of Fox, we began the climb to Cleary Summit. This proved to be our undoing. As we climbed, we penetrated deeper into a cloud bank, and the visibility kept dropping. When we could only see about twenty feet ahead, driving became impossible. I pulled off at the next scenic overlook to turn around. The parking area of the overlook was narrow, but with Gayle directing me from outside the RV, we succeeded, and with a sigh of relief, headed back to Fox.

Upon arriving, we drove to the town's only campsite, and it was closed. Dejected, we looked for a restaurant to mull over what to do next. There were two in town, but both were closed until five o'clock, and the clock on our dashboard told us it was now three. We pulled into Fox's sole gas station and learned that the campsite was closed because its construction violated zoning. I thought to myself, my goodness, they have zoning up here! What a blow this was to my perception that Alaska is America's last bastion of freedom, as it was known to the pioneers. We also learned that no change in the weather was expected tomorrow. Returning to the RV, we mulled over our situation. Our options were to stay in the area and free camp or head South toward Denali National Park. A flip of a coin decided the issue, and we proceeded back up the Steese Highway to look for a place to free-camp for the night.

Five miles up the road, we came upon a flat area where a gold dredge had left its wake along the side of the highway. A small stream named Pedro Creek ran through the middle of the dredge's tailings, and from the holes dug into the stream bank, we could see that other panners had worked this spot. After parking and setting up, Gayle did the panning and I used our metal detector in the hope of finding a sixteen-ounce nugget missed by the dredge. Gold fever does very strange things to people and Gayle and I, apparently, are no exception to this rule.

Pedro Creek and the tailing pile left by Gold Dredge #4. The size of this pile of waste gravel is small, which means the dredge was also small.

Gold dredges are only ninety-five percent efficient extracting gold from their diggings and it was this elusive five percent that we were looking for. The lost five percent is primarily nuggets larger than the screening holes in the dredge's main tumbler. These larger nuggets pass through the dredge with the tailings and are dumped to the rear. Dredge tailings are commonly used to construct highways in Alaska and this probably was the source of the sixteen-ounce nugget that was found on the Elliot Highway.

Gold dredges were truly awesome pieces of equipment. The largest ones had digging buckets 18 cubic feet in size, which could excavate as much as fifteen thousand cubic feet of gravel a day. Each bucket load of dirt typically held one hundred twenty-five milligrams of gold or about three match heads' worth. It took two hundred fifty bucketfuls to mine one ounce of gold. To put all of this in perspective, imagine a pile of rocks two stories high and as big as a football field. That's a huge pile of rocks, but now imagine one hundred piles of rocks this size. This is how much soil and rock were processed by one of the larger dredges in one year.

Another interesting aspect of our present location, which we learned from a sign we found lying face down on the ground, is that this is the spot where Felix Pedro, an immigrant Italian coal miner, first struck gold in 1902. Felix was born in Trignano, Italy, and there his name was Felice Pedroni. Upon immigrating to this country, his prospecting buddies Americanized his name. It was Felix's discovery that led to a gold rush in the area, which resulted in the settlement of Fairbanks. This settlement grew into the city we know today. Like most other placer gold claims in Alaska, after the easy pickings played out, Felix and the other placer miners in the area sold their claims to big companies, and once these companies owned all the claims, they brought in Gold Dredge #4, which decimated the area in its search for gold.

A gold dredge actually is a ship that sails across the ground. Gold Dredge #8, which weighed in at over one thousand tons, was one hundred feet long, fifty feet wide, and was a six-cubic-foot dredge; the volume in cubic feet of its digging buckets. The digging buckets are mounted end to end on a huge blade, like teeth on a chainsaw. The blade on Gold Dredge #8 was about fifty feet long and was capable of reaching thirty feet below the waterline of the dredge.

A gold dredge is basically a barge that floats on a self-dug pond. Its huge buckets do the digging and empty their loads into a perforated rotating steel drum, which is continually flushed with water. On God Dredge #8, the drum is thirty feet long and four feet in diameter. The water washes the dirt and sand through the drum's perforations, carrying the gold with it. This mixture of dirt, sand, silt, and gold is then run over corrugated panels, which capture the gold-laden silt in its grooves. Finally, the gold-rich silt is retrieved and sent to a processing facility where the gold is extracted by washing the silt with mercury. The mercury dissolves the gold, which is recovered in a pure state by distillation.

Seen from above, a gold dredge is a mechanical monster sitting in a self-dug pond. It eats the ground in front and defecates processed ground to its rear. By so doing, the pond and dredge move across the landscape at a slow but steady pace like a huge water beetle. Gold Dredge #8, closed by the EPA and OSHA regulations in 1959, operated for thirty years. During this time, it traveled a distance of four and one-half miles and removed 7.5 million ounces of gold from the ground. From the air, you can still see the indelible scar of its journey across the once pristine Alaskan wilderness. We are presently camped upon a section of a gold dredge scar made by Gold Dredge #4; also known as the Pedro Dredge. I hate to think what Alaska would look like if the government didn't step in and put a stop to this appalling crime against nature.

A gold dredge, if it was not following a stream bed, did not just haphazardly drive around the countryside digging up gold. The route that it traveled was carefully planned ahead of time so that it would be the most productive. In Alaska, dredges only operated two hundred days out of the year during the summer months. Winter snows and icy temperatures put a stop to their operation for the rest of the time. Also, a dredge was not capable of digging up frozen ground, and permafrost or permanently frozen ground is everywhere in Alaska. In order for a dredge to operate, teams of men would proceed ahead of it as much as two years in advance. They thawed the permafrost by driving steel pipes into the ground through which steam was pumped. Once thawed, the ground stayed that way for several years, allowing the dredge to dig down to bedrock.

It rained throughout the night, and I woke up this morning to severe foggy conditions. I was sure the fog would prevent us from making it over Cleary Pass. On the upside, the rain should dampen some of the forest fires in the area. However, we may never make it to Nome Creek. I guess my aspirations of getting rich will have to be satisfied elsewhere in Alaska.

Saturday, August 10, Writing from a free camp on Nome Creek, White Mountain Recreational Area, Population 0

As we were leaving our campsite yesterday, the clouds started to break so we decided to chance Cleary Pass one more time. We had no trouble getting over the pass this time and we traveled up the Steese Highway as originally planned. At mile marker 29, we came upon the Chatanika Lodge; a sprawling and many-roomed log cabin with a bar and restaurant. Across the road, about two hundred yards or so into the bush was Gold Dredge #3, the second largest gold dredge in Alaska. In contrast to the fee we paid yesterday to see Gold Dredge #8, this dredge sits abandoned and can be viewed for free. Our intention is to explore this huge piece of equipment on our way back to Fairbanks.

Cleary Pass on the Steese Highway. This picture was taken on the way back when the weather was much improved from the way in. The line at the center of the mountain to the left is the road we traveled.

At mile marker 44, the pavement ended, and for the first time in our journey, we were on a real Alaskan dirt road. It was two lanes wide and well-maintained. We were now twenty-odd miles from Nome Creek, seven of which would be on a smaller park road of unknown character. The Steese Highway continues on for one hundred twenty more miles past the Nome Creek turnoff and ends in the town of Circle (Population 89). Circle is one of the many places in Alaska with only one road in and the same road out. I'll bet the town is a real jumping place on Saturday night.

Upon arriving at the White Mountain cutoff road, I parked, unloaded the motorcycle, and explored the seven miles of dirt road to Nome Creek. It was a decent one-lane road, far narrower than the Steese Highway, but still usable by an RV. Returning, I told Gayle that the trip would be no problem provided we didn't meet someone heading the other way. We were fortunate in this regard, and this drive taught me another inviolate truth about RV'ing; roads appear much bigger from the seat of a dirt bike as opposed to sitting eight feet up in an eleven-ton motor home.

We arrived at Nome Creek and set up at a spot I had picked on my exploratory visit. The sun was shining and the day was warm. We decided to have lunch before getting rich. By the time we finished, it was drizzling. The rain was of no concern because I was sure it would only take us a few hours of panning to realize our dream. To avoid the rain, we panned under a bridge that crosses over Nome Creek. After an hour or so of hard work, we were still empty-handed. At this point, being too cold to continue, we returned to the RV for an afternoon cocktail. The drizzle continued for the rest of the day. Later, I did some exploring and a little more panning but found nothing worthy of note.

The flattened tailing piles at Nome Creek in the White Mountains Recreational Area.

Tired, we called it day around nine-thirty and looked forward getting rich in the morning. As I gazed out our bedroom window, I watched ground hugging clouds rolling in off the surrounding hills. It rained most of the night and much to my chagrin, we awoke encased in a pea soup fog. It is seven o'clock, Gayle is still asleep, and I have spent the morning watching the fog lift a bit then close back in. Unfortunately, it never lifted high enough to see the tops of the hills we crossed getting here.

Our options are to chance leaving or sit and wait for a break in the weather. By staying, we face a wet and dreary day of doing nothing. We can pan for gold, but it is cold and without the sun, that is not an inviting prospect. My hope is that the clouds will lift sometime during the day so we can leave. Another option is to follow a smaller vehicle back to the main road. Once there, it is a short drive back to the relative luxury of Chatanika Lodge. Right now, I would give all the gold in Alaska to be there.

CHAPTER 8

The Road to Denali

Sunday, August 11, writing from Anderson, Alaska, 79 Miles South of Fairbanks, Population 517

Shortly after Gayle woke up yesterday morning, a local couple happened by. They intended to explore the area using ATV's which they towed behind their camper. Unfortunately, they were also put off by the weather. Alan and Connie were both retired from the U.S. Navy, and being ex-Navy myself, we swapped sea stories and hit it off really well. After expressing my concerns about the fog, Alan agreed to hold point position and lead me through the soup to safety. As we were leaving, the fog lifted somewhat, and we encountered no problems on the way out.

Our drive out of the valley taught me another universal truth about RV'ing: visibility in fog seems far worse on a wide two-lane highway as opposed to a narrow dirt road lined with brush and trees. We also learned from our new friends that the gravel area where we were parked was created by bulldozing flat the tailings of a gold dredge. This dredge could be found abandoned about four miles downstream from where we were. I wish we had time to explore it, but our concern about the weather overrode doing so.

By the time we got back to the Steese Highway, the weather improved, and we began to see patches of blue sky and glimmers of sunlight. As I drove, I wondered what the weather conditions were like back in the valley we had just left. Soon, we were on a paved highway and continued to the Chatanika Lodge for lunch.

The Chatanik Lodge on the Steese Highway.

Chatanika used to be a busy gold mining town, but the town is now gone, and all that is left is the Chatanika Lodge, the abandoned gold dredge, and some derelict buildings from the town's glory days. And I do mean glory! Over 70 million dollars worth of gold was taken out of the ground in the area between 1926 and 1957. The Lodge is now home to the *Chatanika Days Outhouse Race* held in March. The racing outhouses are specially built, un-motorized contraptions powered by four pushers with one person riding and steering. I never found out if the rider was required to use the outhouse during the race.

At the lodge, we met Ralph and his brother. Ralph was celebrating his thirtieth year in Alaska because from this day forward, he would be a *sourdough*. Before today, his status was a "newcomer". It takes thirty years of residency to earn the honorific title of *sourdough.* Sourdough originally referred to early gold rush stampeders who carried with them unbaked lumps of sourdough bread. This slug of dough carried the organisms that gave sourdough its characteristic flavor. They used this dough to make bread that ensured their survival in the gold fields. Upon making more dough, they always saved a lump for the next batch. It was an act of communion for miners to share their prized dough with others.

Ralph also told us where we could find undefiled streams with good color (gold) in them. Apparently, that's the way it is seeking gold in Alaska: you always come by the right information at the wrong time. I also am beginning to think that asking an Alaskan to tell you where to find gold is akin to asking a fisherman to tell you how to find his favorite fishing spot. After all, if someone really knew where gold could be found in quantity, would they be telling you about it?

At this point, I would like to comment on the people we have met. We have not run into any native Alaskans at all, and I am beginning to think that everyone in the state is a transplant. There also seems to be an unusually large number of people from Florida here, and if they are not from Florida, then they have visited the state at one time or another. In any case, all the people we have met have been warm, friendly, and interesting to converse with. It only takes a few words to warm up to them, and there seems to be a strong commonality in their thinking and ours; they don't like other people to tell them what to think and prefer others in small doses.

After lunching at the Chatanika Lodge, Gayle headed for the motor home, and I headed across the road to climb the tailing piles made by Gold Dredge #3. She was a sight to behold, sitting in her self-made pond that stretched off into the wilderness. Apparently, this dredge deposited its tailings off to the side instead of directly to the rear and as a result, left a river-like lake in its wake. The tailing piles had to be at least fifty to sixty feet high.

The tailing piles of Gold Dredge #3, the 2nd largest dredge in Alaska. You can readily see the difference between the output of this dredge and opposed of Gold Dredge #4 on Pedro Creek.

Gold Dredge #3 was in fairly good shape and was half again as big as Gold Dredge #8. I was disappointed because it was floating in its self-dug pond and there was no way I could get to it without swimming. As is usually the case, the dredge's buckets were gone. Many of the smaller buckets from smaller dredges end up being used as decorative planters by the locals. I have no idea what they do with the buckets from a dredge this size.

The second-largest gold dredge in Alaska, stranded forever across the road from the Chatanika Lodge on the Steese Highway.

We drove back to Fairbanks, re-provisioned and headed south down the Parks Highway toward Denali National Park. Ten miles out of Fairbanks we stopped in Ester (Pop. 240); a two-bar town. One of them was the famous Malemute Saloon which is home of the *Service with a Smile* show. The show features songs, poetry, and stories of the early gold rush days. We decided to not stay here because the RV park nearby did not have electricity or water on site. After Nome Creek, we were tired of free camping and wanted a little more civilization than this place offered. After driving twenty-five miles or so, we stopped in the town of Nenana situated on the confluence of the Nenana and Tanana Rivers. Apparently, they go bananas with names around here.

Nenana was supposed to have a decent RV park, but what really got our attention was that most of the town's buildings were wood, and its streets were unpaved dirt. The town looked like something out of the Old West, but its real claim to fame is the *Ice Classic* that it hosts once each year. The Ice Classic is a statewide competition that costs $2.50 to enter. Participants vie to guess the date and time that the Tanana River ice will break up in the spring. The person guessing closest to the actual breakup time wins a purse worth about $300,000. Nenana, believe it or not, used to be called Tortella, which sounds like something Felix Pedro would come up with. However, it really is a shortened version of the Indian word *Toghotthele*, which translates means *mountain that parallels the river*.

We drove down "A" Street in Nenana and turned onto Fourth Avenue, where we were disappointed to find the RV Park closed and for sale. Tired to the point of exhaustion, we drove back to the Parks Highway and headed South to Anderson (Pop. 517). We pulled into the town's Riverside Park and found an RV camping area adjacent to its picnic pavilion. We felt at home here because Gayle and I had lived in the neighborhood of Riverside Park for twenty years, back in Fort Lauderdale.

Today's journey will take us to Denali National Park, where, weather permitting, we will see Mt. McKinley. Mt. McKinley or Denali as it is called by the Athabaskan Indians, is the highest mountain in North America. Its peak soars 20,320 feet above sea level. Denali is so huge that it creates its own weather and even on clear days, its summit may be shrouded in clouds. The mountain is visible only forty percent of the time and seeing it completely free of clouds is a religious experience.

Sunday, August 11th, writing from Riverside RV Park, Denali, Alaska

The road from Anderson was excellent. We pulled off several times to view the scenery and take pictures. Regrettably, one rest area where we stopped was strewn with garbage and trash, despite its readily available trash receptacles. Gayle and I cleaned up as best we could and wondered what kind of animal would do such a thing. There are people who murder, rob banks, and swindle retirees out of their savings; so, what is so bad about a litterbug? From my perspective, the criminals mentioned are deplorable human beings, but at least they admit to who and what they are. A person who litters is also a deplorable human being, but unlike the other criminals, litterbugs have no comprehension of the depth of their depravity. They actually think despoiling the world within which we live is normal and never stop to think that such acts are an affront to God and their fellow human beings.

As we traveled, Gayle pointed out highlights along the way from The *Milepost*. As usual, I always read more into something than most other people and today was no exception. *The Milepost* warns that, northbound, we will be in a moose danger zone for the next twenty-two miles. It is clear from this warning that the Moose are only a threat to those traveling northbound and southbound travelers have nothing to fear. If the moose are only a threat to northbound traffic, then they must have been trained to not cross the road. If the moose have been trained to not cross the road, then they are not wild and probably were placed in the area by the Chamber of Commerce to attract tourists.

Similarly, I have determined that the State of Alaska discriminates against tourists. *The Milepost* also warns us to watch for rough road and dips northbound. If the road is only rough and dippy northbound, then it must be smooth and level southbound. This being the case, it follows that the State of Alaska maintains southbound traffic lanes better than those going north, to the detriment of northbound travelers. Why the state would treat one group of travelers better than another escapes me and from my perspective, doing so is blatant discrimination.

Tomorrow, weather permitting, we will tour Denali National Park by helicopter. Part of the tour includes landing on one of the Park's glaciers where I hope to find a frozen woolly mammoth and fulfill my insatiable desire to taste a well-aged mammoth burger.

Monday, August 12th, writing from Riverside RV Park, Denali, Alaska

We have apparently offended his majesty, the great god Denali, because he has shown us disfavor with clouds and rain. I am sure his displeasure results from the fact that we have approached his flanks without telling you very much about him. All gods hate to be ignored.

Denali, the Athabascan Indian name for Mt. McKinley means *the High One.* Indians are always descriptive when naming something. Denali rises 20,320 feet above sea level, and the surrounding lowlands are only 2,000 feet above sea level. This gives *the High One* a vertical relief of 18,000 feet, which is greater than the vertical relief of Mount Everest, the tallest mountain in the world at 29,035 feet. Winter lows on Denali's summit hover around minus ninety-five degrees, and storm gusts blow as high as one hundred fifty miles per hour. Snow permanently covers seventy-five percent of the mountain, and its slate core is overburdened by ice one hundred fifty feet thick in places.

Mt. McKinley Park was established in 1917, but in the recent wave of *political correctness*, the Park was renamed Denali National Park in 1980. Presently, there are movements afoot to officially rename Mt. McKinley, Denali. Similarly, I hear there are people who are trying to get New York State to rename Long Island, Enoo Yahhayneenoo, which is Iroquois for *Big Fish*, the shape of Long Island from the air. They also want to rename Manhattan Island, *Ka Ellee Sutee Menoonee, aka Sutoobahchanee*, which literally translates means, *we really put one over on the palefaces this time.*

CHAPTER 9

A Denali Adventure

Wednesday, August 14th, Writing from Anchorage, Alaska

I just had an interesting thought. Archaeologists are still trying to figure out how a tribe of uneducated South American Indians was able to turn the plains of Nazca into the World's largest graffiti exhibit. They are stymied because the Indians had no way of viewing the art they created. This being true, I wonder how the resident Indians of lower New York knew that Long Island was shaped like a fish. I surmise they made this determination by jumping off the cliffs of New Jersey in hang gliders.

Presently, we are camped just outside Denali National Park. We retired last night with the setting sun peeking through the clouds. Upon awakening, it was clear that my homage to Denali paid off because the sun was shining and scattered clouds dotted the sky. Before proceeding, I would like to say a word about the town where we are camped; it doesn't exist. To be sure, we see it spread out before us, but from a political and geographic point of view, it does not exist. It is not really a town, a city or even township. What it is according to the college kids who work here is *the strip*. Why this place is a phenomenon and not a geographic place on the map is that everyone, without exception, leaves for the winter. The buildings remain, but all the people are gone. If you want a cup of coffee or to gas up on your way to Fairbanks, you are out of luck.

Our campground just outside Denali National Park on the Nenana River.

We toured Denali National Park by helicopter, but I am sorry to say we did not land on a glacier. The glacier tour took you outside the park, away from Denali, and we chose the tour that took us up close and personal with this great god. Our flight was booked with ERA Helicopters in a six-passenger turbojet-powered helicopter. I am an ex-Naval Jet Fighter Pilot with 230 carrier landings to my credit, so I guess one would assume that I am a fearless kind of guy. However, the truth is that this helicopter ride scared me. In fairness to ERA and our fine pilot, I should point out that Gayle and everyone else onboard loved every minute of the flight.

Gayle and me ready to board our helicopter and visit Denali.

I reacted differently from the others because of my background as a pilot. In a jet airplane, at altitude, forward movement is imperceptible, but you never lose your sense of forward motion. Such is not the case with a helicopter, which is akin to riding in an elevator without cables. Furthermore, the day of our tour was windy, and this meant a significant amount of turbulence due to wind churning over the extreme terrain. When our helicopter encountered this turbulence, it shuddered. If I ever felt a similar shudder in an F-4 Phantom, I would have ejected immediately. Finally, most of the flying I have done was over the ocean or flat terrain. I was unnerved flying over mountains where no place for an emergency landing was evident.

The pad we departed from was on a clearing near the Nenana River, facing a stand of trees rising above us on a mountain slope. We lifted from the pad, drifted backwards and about one hundred feet up, and executed a turn toward Denali National Park. At first, the mountains were low and had no snow on their rounded peaks. The wooded areas on the lower flanks of the mountains, made up of widely spaced permafrost-stunted pine trees, are called taiga. Permafrost is a layer of permanently frozen earth, which in this area is approximately one foot below the surface of the ground. It is this never-melting soil that limits root growth and stunts the growth of the trees we were seeing. At some point up the mountain, dependent upon the slope's orientation to the sun, the taiga turns to tundra. Tundra is made up of mosses, lichens, grasses, low shrubs, and grass-like plants called sedges.

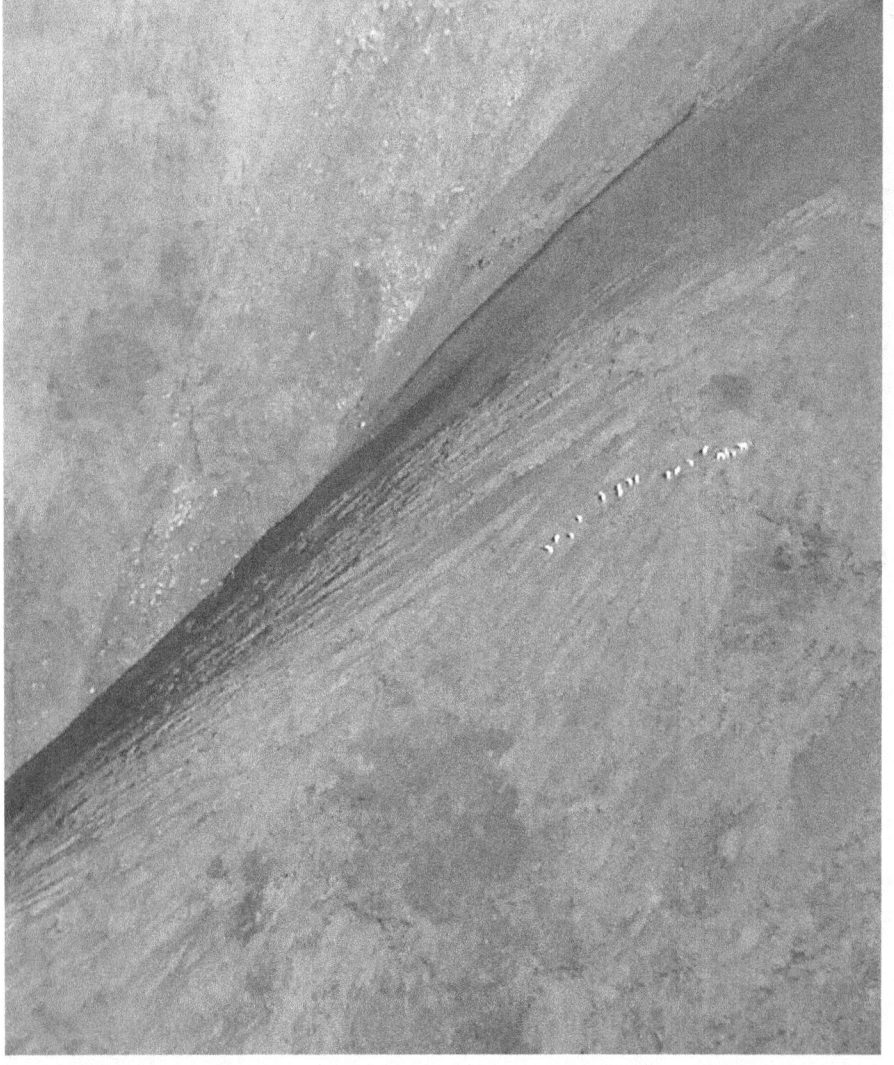

From the vantage point of our helicopter, the tundra looked like newly mowed grass. According to our pilot, if our flight had taken place a few weeks later, those ground-hugging plants would have displayed the same colors worn by the foliage of New England in the fall. What a magnificent sight these mountains must be in their autumn glory.

Looking down at a herd of Dall's sheep from our helicopter.

As we proceeded deeper into the park, the mountains kept getting steeper and higher. The Dall's sheep were everywhere, but we never did see any grizz. On some of the ridges, Dall's sheep and caribou trails were evident and they looked like bicycle paths through the tundra. I envisioned what it would be like to mountain bike these forbidding slopes. As we progressed, snow-covered peaks appeared before us and the mountains below bore evidence of termination dust; a light dusting of snow that is a harbinger of the coming winter. As we proceeded, we flew over several glacier-fed rivers. The rivers were opaque with "glacial flour"; a grey stone dust created by the grinding action of glaciers over the rocks of the mountains. Nothing lives in these rivers because of the choking nature of this noxious mix.

Heading into steeper mountains in our helicopter on the way to Denali.

The termination dust soon turned into snow fields, and finally, as we rounded a snow-covered peak, before us in all his majesty, stood Denali. We were fortunate, his southwest flank was shrouded in clouds and his peak hidden by a rectilinear cloud resulting from jet stream winds, but there he was. The image of his magnificence will be burned into my mind forever. At this point, I shuddered to think what it would be like to make a forced landing in all that vertical ice and snow. I felt like we were riding in a glass elevator, and the only thing keeping us in the air was four rotating fence rails. Talk about the Twilight Zone! Give me a pitching carrier deck on a dark, stormy night, anytime.

We are getting close to Denali. This is a view of an unnamed alpine glacier dropping off into a valley. Imagine doing an emergency landing in this kind of terrain.

After viewing the "High One" and taking pictures, we changed direction and made a rapid descent between the smaller mountains that are the handmaidens to Denali. Denali towers five thousand feet above every other mountain in Alaska. He is alone in his majesty. We descended into a valley bisected by a glacial stream and followed the stream to its source, a massive river of ice inching its way down from the top of the mountain. As we climbed up the slope of this glacier, its turquoise blue ice riveted our attention. A glacier is not frozen water, but instead, fallen snow compressed by its own weight into hard-solid ice. The start of this process, called the accretion zone, is a snow field near the top of the mountain, the glacier's source. The accretion zone of the glacier we were over soon loomed into view, and at the blink of an eye, it was beneath us. Before us, we now beheld a vast snowfield with nothing breaking the pristine whiteness of its surface.

Denali or the "High One", taken from our helicopter. We are about thirty miles from the mountain when this picture was taken. Notice the rectilinear cloud that obscures the mountain's summit. Similar to a jet airplane's contrail, this cloud is made up ice crystals condensing out of jet steam winds.

After landing and returning to reality, we drove the road into Denali National Park for its fifteen-mile paved length; the distance private vehicles are allowed to drive into the park. The scenery, of course, was spectacular. Don't think woods; think taiga; sparsely wooded fields, miles across, sloping up the surrounding mountains to fields of tundra and rounded granite peaks. Words are inadequate to describe the beauty we beheld. Upon reaching the turnaround point, we retraced our steps, left the park, and headed south on the Parks Highway toward Anchorage.

A view from the access road in Denali National Park. Notice the taiga in the foreground and the line of tundra at the base of the mountains in the distance.

CHAPTER 10

The Road to Anchorage

Wednesday, August 14th, Writing from Anchorage, Alaska, Population 260, 263, approximately forty-two percent of the entire State

Once on the Parks highway, our thoughts returned to finding gold and getting rich. According to, *Where to Prospect for Gold in Alaska Without Getting Shot,* we would achieve our goal at milepost 175 (from Anchorage) at Hurricane Gulch. I should have known something was amiss from this name; whoever heard of a hurricane in Alaska? Gold fever can make you gullible to the point of being stupid. We arrived at Hurricane Gulch, and it was readily apparent that a parachute was needed to reach the six-foot-wide stream flowing two hundred sixty feet below its bridge. The stream looked as tiny as the laces on my sneakers. Not only would I need a parachute to get down to it, I would need a fibrillator to assist me on the climb back up.

A mountain view from the Taylor Highway on our way to Anchorage.

With optimism reigning supreme, we proceeded down the road to another get-rich-quick spot called Little Coal Creek (Milepost 162.2). As we passed over the stream's bridge, the torrent below seemed more reachable than the stream at Hurricane Gulch. We stopped at a nearby pull-off, and much to the chagrin of Gayle, I waved goodbye as I peddled away on my bike with as much gold-finding gear as I could carry. Pay dirt was only a few scoops away. Upon reaching the bridge, I was dismayed to see how far below the bridge the stream really was. This wasn't Hurricane Gulch, but the look down still took your breath away.

Coal Creek takes from the bridge on the Taylor Highway that crosses it.

I looked for a trail down to the stream on the right. No luck! I did the same on the left. No luck! I repeated my search across the bridge. Still no luck! Let me now take the liberty of quoting directly from Ron Wendt, *Gold panning, sluicing, 300-foot right-of-way. Check under the road. Rumors abound from this creek*. Doing as directed, I checked under the road, and the altitude made my head swim. At this point, the only rumor I wanted to spread about this creek is that Mr. Wendt is buried somewhere along its banks.

Okay, I'm overreacting! If this creek is so inaccessible, surely it must have gold in it? Eureka, I just figured out another truism about finding gold in Alaska; if you can get there easily, you won't find any. Earlier, upon approaching Little Coal Creek in the RV, I noticed a trail marker indicating a trail that may lead to it. I remounted my bicycle and, with great exertion, pedaled to the trailhead. My intention was to hide my bike when I got there. As I pedaled, I wondered if it would be safe to hide in the woods so near the road.

Upon arriving at the trailhead, it was evident that if I hid my bike as intended, it probably wouldn't be found during my lifetime. While the trail was discernible, the encroaching foliage was so thick that you needed a machete to get through it. Undeterred, I hacked on through this living salad bowl and, after a hundred feet or so, stopped to question my sanity. As I stood in the oppressive silence, it occurred to me that I could not hear the stream I was looking for, even though it sounded like a jet fighter in afterburner at the bridge crossing. At this point, feeling very much like Grizz fodder, I decided I would get rich somewhere else.

On the road again! Where to stop; where to lay our tired heads? According to "The Milepost", at mile marker 121.5, there is a paved/double-ended rest area with tables, fire pits, drinking water, toilets, shade trees, and a lush growth of cow parsnip. This all sounded well and good, but it was the word "lush" that caught my eye and this was the deciding factor for our stopping there. Upon arriving, we were overjoyed because this place turned out to be one of those magical spots you chance upon once every so often.

The rest area was a state park with several roads crossing its length. At the end of each road was a parking area to accommodate RV's or campers. As promised, outhouses were available, but they were not very inviting. Gayle was grateful that we have our own toilet with us. However, as promised, the campground was lush. A short distance from where we parked, I located a picnic table, barbecue grill, and water well, by hacking through the foliage with my machete. The well was equipped with an old-fashioned hand-pump and looked like something out of a farmer Brown cartoon.

The only water available at our campground is on Taylor Highway. Notice the lush foliage and a few fireweed plants on the left.

We parked and leveled the RV. The sun was shining brightly, and we sat there in awe. It was as if we found the Garden of Eden. Trees were everywhere, and we were surrounded by fireweed and cow parsnip that grew higher than our heads. The area was so green it looked like a commercial for Clorets. Fireweed grows everywhere in these northern climes, especially where trees are absent. It is the first foliage to pop up after a forest fire, which gave the plant its name. Its blossoms are a bright purple, and, in the spring, forest fire scorched hills are shrouded under a vivid purple blanket. It truly is a beautiful sight.

The Taylor Highway state campground at marker 121.5, on the road to Anchorage.

I walked the dogs down a trial marked "scenic view" and as I did, I wondered how much of a view I would find. I didn't have to go far to find out. After a hundred yards or so, looking up, it became apparent that I was running out of woods. Blue sky was beginning to dominate the view. I soon heard a river and upon walking several yards further, I realized I was on a ridge overlooking a rapidly flowing river about one hundred feet below where I stood. The drop down to the river was steep and heavily wooded, such that the view was obscured no matter where I stood. I gleefully returned to the RV and fetched Gayle to show her my discovery.

Why RV? What's it all about? Why go to Alaska? Good questions! I think camping in this remote spot at mile marker 121.5, answers them all. First, there was no entry fee to be here, but that is not the point. Here we were, in our beautiful home away from home, at a location unknown to most, even many of the people who live here, and for a short period of time, it was ours. It wasn't part of the United States, and it wasn't part of Alaska. It wasn't a part of any of these man-made artificialities; it was ours. We owned it, lock stock and barrel; and it owned us. That's the important part. By being there, it became a part of us and we became a part of it. This relationship was fleeting, but what isn't in life? The important thing is that it happened, if only for a short period of time and Gayle and I are better off for it. No one who lives in a fixed home and has never RV'ed, will ever be able to imagine what this feels like.

The next morning, we broke camp and headed south on the Parks Highway. After traveling five miles, I noticed a group of people on the shoulder taking pictures. As I passed, I wondered what they were taking pictures of. This road has looked the same for the past 20 miles and I did not see any special reason for stopping there. Passing them, I looked into my rear-view mirror in and the answer to my question was obvious. There in all his glory, framed squarely in my rear-view mirror, stood Denali; naked without any clouds to shield him from view.

Slowing, I found a place to turn around and drove back to join the others paying homage to this magnificent god. The sky was cloudless, unfortunately there was some smoke in the air, but through the haze, there stood Denali, naked for all to see. No clouds and no jet stream; just the sky and the High One. If you ever come to Alaska, see Denali. You will not be the same afterwards.

A view of Denali on the road to Anchorage, eighty miles from the mountain.

The road to Anchorage was excellent. At 50 miles out, civilization overtook us. Blockbuster video, Pizza Shack, Subway, Sears, Safeway, and a divided four lane highway, were all evident. In the blink of an eye, we had left Alaska and returned to the United States. Please understand that I am grateful to these fine corporations for the bounty they give us, it's just that when I fall down upon my knees in reverence, I prefer to do it to Denali and not them.

CHAPTER 11

The Road to Homer

Saturday, August 17th, Writing from the Kenai Peninsula, Sterling Highway, Peterson Lake Campground, Pop.

We stayed in Anchorage for three nights, catching up on personal business. Anchorage is an interesting city that retains some of the flavor of its frontier beginnings. However, the traffic at rush hour is horrible. Downtown is typical of any big city, with store-lined streets and buildings climbing to eight stories. We visited American Legion Post 29, where Chuck, the State Commander, and Dean, the State Adjutant, engaged us in the usual Legion game of seeing who could buy the other the most drinks. They were gracious and informative.

Anchorage welcomes us through the windshield of our motor home.

The American Legion is more active in Alaska than in the lower forty-eight, because many ex-military personnel settle here after leaving the service. Retired military personnel also make up a large percentage of the overall population and as a result, the average age of legion members in Alaska is lower than in most other states.

This morning, after making reservations to go halibut fishing in Homer, we headed south on the Seward Highway. The ride, like most drives in Alaska, was a pleasant surprise. After the scenery we have seen over the past few weeks, we thought nothing more would impress us. The first stretch of the Seward Highway heads southeast along the Turnagain Arm of Cook Inlet. Initially, it is a four-lane road that runs beside the inlet. We were transiting at dead low tide so the mud flats were exposed and they extended away from shore for miles. According to "The Milepost", walking them is risky because of the deep mud and the fact that when the tide comes in, it does so faster than a man can run on solid ground.

Picture 78 – A view of the mud flats from the Seward Highway south of Anchorage.

As we drove along Seward Highway, to the North were mountains with snow fields and glaciers rivaling those in Jasper National Park. The scenery was beautiful. Snow-capped mountains to the left and a picturesque inlet bordered by snow-capped mountains on the right. One overlook in particular is noted for visits by white beluga whales, which, on occasion, come into the inlet to feed. They usually visit in July, so we were too late to see them.

Forty-six miles from Anchorage, the Seward Highway bends around the inlet and heads southwest. At this point, the Bore Tides, as they are called, are thirty-three feet from top to bottom and roll in as foaming waves six feet high. Time was not with us, and we did not get to see this phenomenon. Hopefully, we will be more fortunate on the way back.

The Seward Highway winds across the northern part of the Kenai Peninsula and is noted for its gold-bearing streams. As we drove, my brain returned to thoughts of getting rich. At milepost 61.7, the road crosses Bertha Creek. You may remember Bertha; she is one of the Butt sisters. Bertha Creek is a two-star gold-bearing stream according to Where to Prospect for Gold in Alaska Without Getting Shot. Upon arriving, we were pleased to see that it was adjacent to a federal campground and that access to the creek would be easy. This morning, I woke up with a slight cold, and although finding gold overshadowed all other considerations, I was not very ambitious. Thank goodness it is warm and sunny.

We parked on the camp road, a short walk to the creek, and were elated to find ideal gold panning conditions: a flat, calm area at the bottom of foaming rapids. I gathered our gear and, with Gayle in tow, headed to the creek that would soon pay off the note on our motor home. Gayle does not take well to trudging through mountain streams or digging pay dirt out of ice-cold water, so our modus operandi was for her to sit on a rock and pan through a five-gallon bucket of gold-bearing gravel that I dug for her. While she did her thing, I used the metal detector to search for big nuggets.

Gayle, panning for gold on Bertha Creek with John Jr. struggling to set up his portable gold dredge in the background.

After an hour or so, it became evident that my metal detector was not working properly, and neither was Gayle's, because we were still empty-handed. About this time, John and John Jr. came on the scene, dragging a motorized five-inch suction pump and a four-foot-long gold sluice with them. They were as new to this game as us, but judging by their equipment, they were a lot more serious about it than we were. A five-inch suction pump can move more gravel in ten minutes than we could pan all day. I remarked to Gayle that I was glad to see that at least someone was going to find something today, and we went back to our panning and detecting.

As I walked, swinging my metal detector from side to side, a shape in the water caught my eye. Not more than eight feet away, I saw a four-foot-long king salmon resting in a pool of slack water. She was a sight to behold, and I thought about grabbing her with my hands. I tried to get closer, but she came to life and swam away. Darn, no gold, and I just missed our supper.

Two more hours passed without any luck. Tired and not wanting to push myself too far, we decided to quit. As we gathered our gear to leave, novices that they were, John and his son were still struggling to set up their equipment in the rapidly flowing creek. We waved them goodbye and good luck. I am sure that if they ever got their equipment set up properly, they would probably find something, but we will never know if they did.

Eventually, we turned off the Seward Highway, which proceeds on to the town of Seward, and turned onto the Sterling Highway, heading for Homer. Homer is about two hundred twenty miles from Anchorage by road and half that distance as the crow flies. Its claim to fame is that it is *the halibut fishing capital of the world*. At present, we are free camping at a public campground on Peterson Lake, about a mile or so off the Sterling Highway. We are sharing this campground with some local families and their kids.

A view of Peterson Lake from our campground on the Kenai Peninsula.

Tomorrow, we have a two-hour ride to Homer, where we will spend the remainder of the day preparing to catch *butt*. *Butt* is short for halibut and a halibut is a big flounder. The record for one on a rod and real is 458 pounds. The all-time record halibut, caught by a commercial fishing vessel, weighed in at 900 pounds. I wondered how they got a fish that big into a frying pan.

CHAPTER 12

A Homer Adventure

Sunday, August 18th, Writing from Homer, Alaska, Population 4,154

Homer sits on the southernmost point of a thumb off the Kenai Peninsula. To the south is a second thumb stretching out into the Gulf of Alaska. The backbone of this second thumb is the Kenai Mountain Range. The body of water that separates the two thumbs is Kachemak Bay, and from our position, it is about ten miles across. Homer is a small town situated on the side of a hill overlooking the bay. At the bottom of the hill is a narrow tongue of land called the spit, which pokes several miles out into the bay.

The Ocean View campground just outside of Homer, Alaska, looking across Kachemak Bay to the Kenai Mountain Range.

At the end of the spit is a manmade lagoon that serves as a harbor for the numerous fishing vessels that ply their trade on Cook Inlet. We will be on one of these boats tomorrow. I am presently sitting at a picnic table next to our RV. It is a warm sunny day and from my perch I have a panoramic view of the bay. To my left, I can see the spit and directly across from me are the snow-capped Kenai Mountains. When god made heaven, He must have used this place as a pattern.

Tomorrow we fish Cook Inlet. My hope is that Homer lives up to its reputation and that there is more fish in Cook Inlet than gold in Bertha Creek.

Monday, August 19th, Writing from Homer, Alaska

Our alarm woke us up at five in the morning and we turned on the television to get the weather. Outside, the sky was cloudy with blue patches of sky poking through the clouds. The weather mavens predicted a cold front approaching from the north which would pass through the area by early evening. The temperature outside was around fifty degrees. I put on my underwear, a set of waffle weaves, jeans, shirt, jacket, and a rain slicker. Gayle dressed in a similar manner and we hopped on our bike (the one with the motor) and drove to Homer Spit.

The drive out to Homer Spit.

We were early getting there. Our fishing partners for the day soon showed up; Tim, his wife Debbie, and their daughter Sarah. Shortly thereafter, Keith, our captain arrived. Instead of being a crusty sailor with a peg leg and patch over his eye, he looked like a school teacher. Introducing himself, it turned out he was a school teacher and charter fishing was only a sideline.

A picture of business establishments on Homer Spit. Our fishing charter was out of the building with the bull's eye on the right side of the picture.

We walked to the boat-filled harbor. It was low tide, and the high-water mark loomed twenty feet above the present water level. Keith's boat was the Celestial Sea, a twenty-seven-foot custom-built aluminum craft powered by twin 150 HP outboards. One look at this vessel gave me the confidence I needed for the day's adventure. After boarding, Keith fired up the engines, and we headed west for an hour or so at twenty-five knots. We passed numerous sea otters and puffins along the way.

A view of the harbor on Homer Spit. Notice the vertical drop of the tide, which was not at full low when this picture was taken.

We followed the Kenai Mountains out to Cook Inlet, rounded a corner, and then proceeded south for another one-half hour. We dropped anchor in eighty feet of water a half mile from shore. Three other charter boats were in view. As Keith helped rig our poles, he explained that this is where we would find the "big ones" and added that if we didn't have any luck here, we would head further out into the inlet to *the mountain*. According to Keith, the mountain was our ace in the hole because over it, we were sure to catch our legal limit of two halibut per person for the day.

The rigs we were using were 6.0 Penn reels with braided 80 lb test line mounted on short fiberglass boat poles. The leader was a 3/16-inch nylon line about 5 feet long with a 2 lb lead sinker attached at its midpoint. In case you think this is a typo, let me reassure you that I said a two (2) pound lead sinker. The hook was 3/16-inch-thick and 3 inches in diameter. It looked more like a gaff than a hook. For bait, we were using whole three-quarter-pound herring. The only time I have seen anyone in Florida rig like this is when they were fishing for monster sharks off the beach. If you know anything about fishing, then you know how much work it will be cranking that amount of weight up to check the bait.

We dropped our rigs over the side, and they went straight down, confirming my suspicion that the amount of weight we were using was unnecessary. The hook itself must have weighed half an ounce. After about ten minutes with no bites, Keith suggested we move away from shore, where there is more current so our bait would move and give off a longer scent trail.

After reeling up, I relished the thought of watching Keith pull up our anchor, a chore I did for years on my buddy Mike's boat. However, to my surprise, instead of pulling up the anchor by hand, Keith started the engines and pulled forward on the anchor line. As he did, the line ran through a one-way fitting on the bottom of the anchor buoy, pulling the anchor up with it. Once the anchor was resting against the bottom of the buoy, it was an easy lift to get the anchor and buoy into the boat. I felt stupid; all those years of arm-breaking labor could have been avoided by purchasing forty dollars' worth of gear.

We moved several hundred yards out into the inlet and dropped our rigs to the bottom in about one hundred feet of water. It was immediately evident that the current was much stronger here because my two-pound sinker would not hold bottom. Keith told us to pull up and switch to a three-pound sinker (groan). After deploying our rigs again, Sarah got the first bite. Sarah is an attractive girl, tall and of slight build. A weight lifter she was not, so it came as no surprise when she quickly tired of hauling up her fish. She struggled for about ten minutes and then her father had to take over. Watching the action, I was amazed when a shape that seemed to be the size of a closet door rose to the surface.

Sarah had hooked a respectable thirty-five-pound Halibut, which Keith deftly gaffed and hauled into the boat. As this monster thrashed about and bounced into the air off the deck, Keith in jest, yelled for Sarah to sit on it. The look on her face told me she would rather jump overboard and before she could move, Keith had the fish by the tail and was savagely, but humanely, beating it over the head with a club. After several blows, the fish went limp into quiet submission. At this point, any reservations I had about having a school teacher for a charter captain quickly evaporated.

We fished for another thirty minutes and had several hits, which precipitated a dreaded crank back to the surface of our three-pound rigs to check bait. Finally, I got a bite, pulled up to set the hook and knew I had something big, because I was having more trouble reeling it up than Sarah had with her fish. Upon surfacing the monster on my line, our excitement immediately faded. I had hooked a twenty-five-pound Skate and it was difficult to pull up because the position of my hook in its mouth made me pull him broadside through the water. We fished for another hour with no luck. The other boats had left some time ago and Keith suggested that we join them on the mountain.

As we turned away from shore, we could see the other boats as specks on the horizon and to my dismay, there were rain clouds where they were. This was of no concern to Keith and he explained that *the mountain* was a huge rise in the bottom of Cook Inlet where the fish congregated. The depth over the mountain averaged two hundred feet and the surrounding terrain sunk down twice that depth. Because of the depth of water and current it would be impossible to anchor. Our modus operandi was going to be to drift over the mountain, fishing as we went.

On our first pass, I hauled in a twenty-five-pound halibut and Gayle caught one a little smaller. We made five passes and caught at least one halibut each time. We also hooked a ten-pound Codfish which, to my dismay, Keith cut up for bait. By the time we were finished, my arms were ready to fall off. We had ten fish, the limit for the five people aboard and they weighed in at two hundred and twenty-five pounds. Filleted, they would be half that much. The rain had picked up and so did the wind. It was time to head home.

The action on the Celestial Sea over the mountain in Cook Inlet.

The seas were now four to six feet with an occasional eight-footer mixed in. Keith's boat was well suited to these waters so this sea state was of no concern. We ran at slow speed for about one hour before the shapes of the mountains loomed into view. As we approached the leeward side of land, the sea became flatter and we were able to pick up the pace. About halfway home we stopped at an island to watch a heard of sea lions relaxing on the rocks. What huge beasts! To our delight four of these magnificent animals surfaced about fifty yards from us. After watching them for a while, Keith started the engines and we continued home.

Sea lions lounging on the rocks in Kachemak Bay.

Upon arriving dockside, a truck was there to take our catch back to the office area where they would be strung up for pictures. After getting pictures, the fish were taken down and filleted. Gayle and I ended up with forty-five pounds of fillets, forty of which we mailed to family and friends. It is not cheap to send forty pounds of frozen fish to the lower forty-eight. The vacuum packing, flash freezing and mailing was about the same as the charter fee for our boat. Imagine if I hauled in a five-hundred-pound fish. I would have had to refinance the RV just to get the fillets home.

Our catch of the day, two-hundred twenty-five pounds of halibut, strung up at the charter rental office on Homer Spit.

After making arrangements to have our catch shipped to friends and family, Gayle and I drove through a cold rain back to the warmth and safety of our motor home. Upon arriving, Scooter and Sally gave us "hell" for leaving them so long, but they were quickly calmed down by an offering of dog treats. I turned up the thermostat and we shed our wet clothes. After relaxing with a well-earned rum coke, I asked Gayle to fry the cheek muscles from the fish we caught. They were a tad grainy in texture but the flavor was excellent. Hopefully, the fillets will be better.

Rain is forecast for the next two days and our intentions are to leave tomorrow and make our way back towards Anchorage.

CHAPTER 13

Encounter With a Glacier

Wednesday, August 21st, Writing from Anchorage Alaska

Last night we stayed at Peterson Lake, the same place where we camped on the way down to Homer. What a beautiful spot. Because it was a weekday, we hoped we would have the place to ourselves. Luck was not with us, and we shared the campsite with three other vehicles. Sometimes, even in Alaska, it is not possible to get away from other people.

Upon getting to Anchorage and after re-provisioning at Freddie Meyers, a local Walmart, we went back to the same RV Park where we had stayed in previously. We needed a sense of belonging at this point, and returning to the campground where we had been before made us feel like we were getting back home. Not having had much of a breakfast, Gayle and I decided to try a halibut filet for lunch. To properly judge our catch, we decided to cook one "straight up", so to speak. Gayle wrapped the filet in tinfoil, added some lemon, butter, basil, and a touch of seasoned salt, and I cooked it on the grill over a medium flame for fifteen minutes. It was excellent! The taste and texture were like fresh-caught grouper, and the meat so tender, it fell apart at the touch of a fork. The filet had no fishy taste at all.

We intend to spend the rest of our time in Anchorage planning our final moves in Alaska.

Saturday, August 24th, Writing from Chicken, Alaska, Population 37

Before proceeding on our journey, there are three subjects that may be of interest to the reader.

Bugs: Bugs have not been bad at all. No-see-ums are non-existent and black flies rare. Mosquitoes have been around, but have not been bothersome enough to stop us from anything we were doing. In one area, while strolling through the woods, they were a challenge, but once out of the woods and in the open, they were no longer a problem. During our entire journey, the biggest problem we have had from bugs was cleaning them off the front of the RV after a day's drive. I have bagged so many of them this way, that I am sure the state will be bug free in a few more days.

Bears: We stayed approximately one week in the Anchorage/Kenai Peninsula area and during that time, three incidents with bears were reported in the local paper.

The first incident involved a man gathering firewood along a stream bank. He inadvertently made the mistake of getting between a sow and her cub. When he realized the dire position he was in, he ran for his life with the sow in hot pursuit. In these situations, I am told that the best thing to do is drop to the ground and play dead. Sure! Anyone can easily lie down and play dead with an enraged five-hundred-pound grizzly charging them. In any case, instead, the man stopped, turned, waved his arms and frantically yelled as loud as he could. Fortunately, the sow with her cub out of danger stopped her charge and retreated.

In the second incident, a young man and his mother where hiking a wilderness trail, turned a blind corner, and confronted a sow grizz, also with a cub. The sow attacked and bit the man on the arm. He dropped to the ground in pain and the enraged bear turned on his mother. The man, regaining his senses, charged the menacing brute screaming and making as much noise as he could. Fortunately, this display was sufficient to convince the bear to retreat.

In the final incident, a man was fishing with his buddies, somewhat separated on a riverbank. Unprovoked and for no apparent reason, a bear came out of the woods and charged him (perhaps this guy stole the bear's favorite fishing spot). Having no time to reach for his rifle, he dove in the river with the bear in hot pursuit. Fortunately, his friends were close enough to help, and they shot and killed the bear, thus saving the man's life.

These incidents occurred in a seven-day period of time and in just one area of the state. Seasonally, there are ten to twenty bear incidents in Alaska and unfortunately, some of them are fatal. The moral of these stories is that bears are not something to be trifled with and in Alaska; humans are just a link in the food chain, not sitting on its top.

Guns: The tragedy that occurred on 9/11 has changed the world in many ways, and most people are not aware of many of these changes. Before 9/11, for a fee, you could transport rifles and handguns through Canada on your way to Alaska. After 9/11, and because of it, handguns are now prohibited. Before learning this, it was my intention to bring a WWII vintage M-1 Carbine and a government-issue 45-Caliber automatic pistol along for protection. Because of the new restrictions, to my chagrin, I had to leave the pistol at home.

As you already know, my primary mode of exploring remote areas in Alaska is the dirt bike mounted on the back of our motor home. It is in these remote areas where a weapon is needed the most for protection from bears and possibly other large animals. In case you're wondering which ones, imagine how being run over by a rampaging 1,800-pound bull moose would feel. An M-1 carbine is a relatively small and light weapon, but despite this, it is still not wise to carry one on an off the road motorcycle. This meant that unless I bought a pistol when I got to Alaska, I would have to brave traveling to wilderness areas without a weapon to protect Gayle and me from bears. I guess this is what one would call a small inconvenience, but it is just one of the many ways that 9/11 has affected our lives and taken away a measure of our freedom.

We left Anchorage, after lingering to clean up some personal business. As we drove the first twenty miles through relatively populated areas, I was melancholy because we were on the last leg of our journey and thought everything else was going to be anticlimactic. This just goes to show how wrong one can be. The scenery, as usual, was magnificent; perhaps better than ever. I have now realized another truism about traveling in Alaska. The scenery is so spectacular everywhere that what you presently view is always the best because no memory, no matter how recent, can match the reality of the moment.

Forty-two miles out of Anchorage we came up the town of Palmer. Palmer is centrally located in the center of the lush farmlands of the Matanuska Valley and it is home to about five thousand people who earn their livings primarily by fishing and farming. Palmer is also home to about two hundred musk oxen, the under wool of which is knitted into garments by native women in rural villages. However, Palmer's main claim to fame is that the Alaska State Fair is held there yearly at the end of August. And what a state fair it is. While the growing season in Alaska is a relatively short three months, the fertility of the soil in the Matanuska Valley is extraordinary. This, combined with the exceptionally long periods of daylight during the Alaskan summer, allows the farmers in Palmer to grow extremely large fruits and vegetables.

Perhaps the most famous farmers in Palmer are John and Mary Evans, who hold seven world records for giant vegetables and two hundred first-place awards at the Alaska State Fair. Among their more spectacular accomplishments are a 70 lb. cabbage, a 43 lb. beet, a 35 lb. Broccoli, a 27 lb. stalk of celery, a 29 lb. kale, a 31 lb. cauliflower, a 71 lb. swiss chard, and a 37 lb. zucchini. All and all, Mike and Mary grow over eighty different varieties of vegetables on their farm. Mike Evan's attributes his success to years of experimentation to get the right combination of soil, seed, and nutrients. Remarkably, Mike's giant vegetables are as flavorful as normal-sized vegetables. "They grow so fast," Evans explains, "they don't have the chance to develop pulp and then lose their flavor." The Palmer's have turned their expertise into a home-grown business and now market their seeds, nutrients, and growing techniques worldwide over the internet.

About eighty miles out of Anchorage, we started to catch glimpses of Matanuska Glacier. Matanuska Glacier is different from most other glaciers in Alaska because its terminus rests on a valley floor, not on a mountain ledge like alpine glaciers. Matanuska glacier is twenty-four miles long, averages two miles in width, and is four miles wide at its terminus. What a magnificent sight from a distance, but what a truly stupendous sight close up.

A distant view of Matanuska Glacier on the Glenn Highway, just north of Anchorage.

A close view of Matanuska Glacier. The expanse of white ice of the terminus is almost four miles across.

We drove the RV to a parking area at the foot of the terminus and I climbed it flanks to the top of its blue ice field. A glacier looks blue because the snowfall that created it is so densely packed by gravity that the entire spectrum of light is absorbed with the exception of blue light. Because the blue light is reflected, this is the color you see when you look at the glacier. What a thrill standing on top the terminus of this glacier this was, especially when I spotted some woolly mammoth bones sticking out of the ice.

The terminus of Matanuska Glacier.

Upon approaching this long-sought find, it became evident that I was too late. Someone had picked the bones clean and nearby there was evidence of a campfire. Darn! This probably was the last frozen woolly mammoth in Alaska and someone beat me to it. Dejected but curious, I scooped up some of the coals and sent them to the University of Alaska for analysis. Later, I learned that they were 10,000 years old. I was confused by this revelation because under the coals, I had also found a partially burned piece of paper upon which you could still make out the words *Sara Lee*. I am beginning to wonder about this state; trained wild animals, bogus gold bearing streams, and now phony archeological sites. I think the Chamber of Commerce definitely is out of control.

The truth of the matter is that I don't think the bones I found were really mammoth bones either. I did a little research and found out that it takes two-hundred and fifty years for a snowflake that fell upon the Glacier's accretion zone twenty-four miles back up into the mountains, to reach its terminus and melt. Talk about slow going, that baby is zipping along at about one mile every ten years. Matanuska Glacier, similar to every other glacier in the world, is shrinking and growing shorter. Many scientists attribute this phenomenon to global warming. I don't know if this is really true or not, but it is a fact that the terminus where we stood was a mile or so further down its valley several years ago.

After viewing Matanuska Glacier, we proceeded up the Glenn Highway towards Tok, which, upon arrival, would complete the nine-hundred-mile circuit around the Great Alaskan Triangle. We free-camped for the night, halfway to Tok in clear view of snowcapped Mount Drum (12,010 feet high) and Mount Sanford (16,237 feet high). Ho Hum! In the morning, we completed the journey to Tok, re-provisioned, and embarked upon the Taylor Highway to Chicken, Alaska, where we are sure to find GOLD.

A mountain view from the Glenn Highway between Tok and Anchorage.

A wilderness view from the Glenn Highway between Tok and Anchorage.

A view of Mount Sanford from the Glenn Highway, adjacent to the turn-off where we free camped for the night.

A view of the pine forested hills from the Taylor Highway between Tok and Chicken, Alaska.

We are presently in Chicken camped in the Original Chicken Gold Camp/Chicken Creek Outpost; an RV park that is also an active gold mine. The park and gold claim are owned by Mike Bushby, a local entrepreneur and miner. About one  hundred yards away from where we are parked is Gold Dredge #4 which is also known as the Pedro Dredge. This is the same dredge that mined Pedro Creek just north of Fairbanks where we had camped earlier in our journey. I guess it's a small world even in a big state like Alaska.

The Chicken Outpost. Our motor home is parked lust to the left immediately behind the camp store. The gold panning area is to the left of our motor home and in the picture looks like a bunch of picnic tables.

Downtown Chicken, Alaska.

Gold Dredge #4 or the Pedro Dredge is a three cubic foot dredge originally owned by the Fairbanks Exploration Company, a subsidiary of the United States Smelting Refining & Mining Company. The dredge was built specifically to mine the shallow gravels of Pedro Creek. It was assembled there in 1938 and mined the Creek until 1958, at which point it ran out of productive streambed. At a cost of $148,000, the dredge was disassembled and reassembled on Chicken Creek in Chicken Alaska in 1959. The dredge actively worked Chicken Creek until it was abandoned in 1967. During that period time, the Pedro Dredge recovered fifty-five thousand ounces of gold from the ground.

Pedro Gold Dredge #4 in the Original Chicken Gold Camp. The pipes in the foreground are water supply and return pipes for the present gold mining operation in the camp.

Pedro Dredge sat where it was abandoned on Chicken Creek until 1998. In that year, the dredge was move one mile by Mike Busby and friends, to where in now sits in Mike's Chicken Creek Outpost and Gold Camp. Amazingly, and much to his credit, the one-million-pound dredge was moved in one piece to its new home with only two weeks of preparation for the move. It took another two weeks to actually make the move. Mike used one-hundred automobile tires to support the dredge during the operation. He never did tell me where he got the tires and what he did with the tires after he was through with them.

Dredging buckets from Pedro Dredge #4. Notice the flowers growing in the rear two bucks. This is the usual fate of most of the dredging buckets reclaimed throughout the state.

There are three gold dredges accessible in the Chicken area. The Pedro Dredge in Chicken proper, the Mosquito Fork Dredge which is a twenty-minute walk on the Mosquito Fork Hiking Trails two miles north of Chicken on the Top of the World Highway, and the Jack Wade Dredge which is alongside the Top of the World Highway about 20 miles north of Chicken. The Jack Wade Dredge or gold dredge #1 is the first dredge used in the area. It used to be called the Butte Creek Dredge when it worked that stream before being moved to Wade Creek. These three dredges are of the smaller variety and can be viewed and explored free of charge.

The Jack Wade Gold Dredge as it sits adjacent to the Top of the World Highway. The dredge is a relatively small one and as it sits is in pretty bad shape.

Upon first arriving at the Chicken Creek Outpost, we talked to a couple that had been panning their all day. They proudly showed us their stash, which they kept in a small glass vial. It wasn't much considering how long they had been panning, but we were thrilled to see it. For the first time in our travels, we were actually looking at real gold that had just been panned out of the ground. The best part was that we would not have to dig the gold-bearing gravel ourselves. We just had to pan through a pile of dirt conveniently placed next to several rows of split fifty-five-gallon drums filled with water. This arrangement proved to be a blessing. The panning drums were waist-high, and this meant you could pan standing up. Panning for gold in a stream is back breaking labor primarily because you are working in a crouched position or on your knees.

It was late in the day, so gold panning had to wait until tomorrow. Tonight, we intend to party in the *world-famous* Chicken Creek Saloon.

CHAPTER 14

Chicken Alaska

Wednesday, August 28th, Writing from Dawson City, Yukon, Canada, Population 2019

Why is Chicken, Alaska, named Chicken? In the early days of the Alaskan gold rush, food was scarce, so miners hunted and ate a plentiful local bird called a ptarmigan. This bird is now the Alaskan state bird. In any case, a ptarmigan resembles a chicken, and when it came time to name the town, they wanted to name it Ptarmigan. However, the miners could not agree on how to spell the name, so in compromise, they settled on Chicken.

Incidentally, the milepost listed the population of Chicken, Alaska, as being thirty-seven people. What's in a number, and who decides what will be counted? According to most of the people I talked to, about fifteen or so brave souls live in Chicken year-round, and, ignoring tourists, miners working their claims swell this number to around one hundred people during the summer months. Chicken is not a nice place to be in the wintertime, unless of course, you are comfortable being with yourself and a few other good people.

What a cast of characters we met in Chicken; both local and imported. Amy, the bartender, hails from California and is a twenty-five-year-old knockout. Being single and pretty, she gets a lot of attention. We also met four guys traveling on motorcycles who had some interesting stories to tell. Then there was George, a local miner who, in the grand old tradition, could tell more stories about Alaska than you can find in a library.

One of the motorcycle riders was an airline pilot by trade and had just returned from a visit to Prudhoe Bay, on Alaska's North Slope. This is an easy thing to say with words and doesn't sound like much, until you realize that the road to Prudhoe Bay begins in Fox, Alaska, the small town we visited just North of Fairbanks, and from there it is a four-hundred-and-fifty-mile drive north through the Alaskan wilderness. Prudhoe Bay lies about two hundred fifty miles north of the Arctic Circle. You have to cross the Brooks Mountain Range to get there.

We panned for gold for two days in Chicken. We were fortunate because we did not have to dig the gold-bearing dirt and gravel directly out of the ground, but this is not to say that all of the digging was eliminated. The first part of the gold retrieval process is to filter the pay dirt from the larger rocks and debris. This is accomplished by using a five-gallon bucket with a plastic mesh lid designed for this purpose. The mesh lid is filled with pay dirt which is then washed through the mesh with water.

Gayle panning for gold at the Chicken Creek Outpost. Notice our RV in the background on the right side of the picture and the pile of gold-bearing soil and gravel in the foreground to the left. The thin line climbing from left to right on the hill in the background of the picture is the Top of the World Highway.

When the bucket is half full of dirt, a portion of it is scoped into a pan which is then swirled to eliminate the pebbles and sand. At the end of the panning process, a small amount of fine black silt is left behind and if you are lucky, flakes of gold will be evident in the silt. These flakes are retrieved with a plastic squeeze bottle that inevitably sucks up some of the silt. Final cleaning will come later in the warmth and comfort of our motor home.

The final cleaning of the gold is a time-consuming process which begins by emptying the contents of the squeeze bottle back into the gold pan. Next, a small amount of water is added and swirled around to spread out the silt and gold flakes. Using tweezers, the bigger flakes of gold are picked out and deposited in a vial. Next, the finer specks of gold are sucked up with an eyedropper, avoiding as much of the silt as possible. The contents of the eyedropper are deposited on a clean white dinner plate, which is swirled to spread out the silt and gold. Next, using a magnifying glass, the remaining specks of gold are separated from the silt by pushing them to the edge of the plate with a sewing needle. After the specks dry, they are carefully pushed over the plate's edge onto a creased piece of white paper which enables you to pour them into a glass storage vial. Using this procedure, it is possible to recover gold flakes smaller than a grain of sand. Without a magnifying glass, these tiny specks do not even look like gold.

After two days of hard work, we ended up with several grams of gold worth around twenty dollars. Gayle, now proudly wears this bounty around her neck in a see-through locket bought at the camp store. Another lesson I learned on this trip is that, as far as getting rich by panning for gold in Alaska is concerned, you may as well stay home and pan for it in your backyard. Your chances of succeeding are about the same. However, you won't have as much fun, and after all is said and done, the real treasure we found was in the experiences we had.

We left Chicken yesterday by way of the "Top of the World Highway," which turned out to be another wonderful segment of our journey. The mountain views were stupendous, spectacular, and never-ending. Most highways follow valleys and riverbeds because their construction is easier on the relatively level terrain. However, to reach the next river or valley, a highway has to climb over a mountain pass or ridge. It is here where one encounters those long steep climbs and descents and is here where the vistas become most spectacular.

A view of the Chicken area from the beginning of the Top of the World Highway. The Chicken Creek Outpost is to the left of center; downtown Chicken just to the right of center, and the Pedro Gold Dredge #4 is to the right of center.

The Top of The World Highway, formerly known as the Ridge Highway, travels from Chicken, Alaska, to Dawson City, Yukon, a distance of one hundred ten miles, almost entirely upon mountain ridges and peaks. For the first twenty miles out of Chicken, the road, typically, follows a river. After that, you climb into the mountains and stay three to four thousand or more feet above sea level for the rest of the journey. Our average speed on this dirt and gravel highway was about fifteen miles per hour. I rarely took the RV out of second gear and I had to use first gear on many of the steeper grades. When the drop-off was on Gayle's side of the RV, she was too afraid to look and kept here face buried in a book. Guard rails were non-existent.

The Top of the World Highway runs back from our motor home along a ridge we had just crossed.

A mountain view from the Top of the World Highway.

As we approached the Canadian border, we came upon Boundary Lodge, one of the first roadhouses in Alaska. Other than the border itself, this is the historic site we will visit in Alaska, and seeing its store and sod roofed bar was a fitting way to conclude our journey. We came to Alaska to experience its untamed wilderness and secluded isolation. This roadhouse and bar, sitting beside the road, miles from nowhere, taught us all we needed to know about isolation.

Boundary Lodge on the Top of the World highway.

The Boundary Lodge Bar, a one-room bar with a sod roof.

A view from the Top of the World Highway, near the Canadian border.

CHAPTER 15

The End of a Dream

Somewhere along the Top of the World Highway, we crossed into Canada, leaving Alaska behind. This great state lived up to all my expectations and it truly is a land of contrasts; a midnight sun and a sun that never rises; winters with below zero temperatures and warm balmy summers; the highest snow-capped mountain peaks and the deepest lush green valleys; wilderness galore and bustling population centers; sparse tundra areas and dense rain forests that produce giant fruits and vegetables.

The only thing Alaska lacked before people arrived on the scene was something to contrast with its great beauty. However, man in his capacity for good and evil has taken care of that. Crime is a problem, gold dredges have left huge scars across the landscape, and the ugliness of discarded garbage and trash at highway pull-offs is all too evident. The saving grace of the state is the terrible Alaskan winter which keeps most people from moving there.

From the perspective of the planet we live on, mankind does two things; he consumes and pollutes. Throughout history, because populations were small, our planet was able to accommodate these nefarious doings. Unfortunately, today, population growth is such that this is no longer the case. We are living on borrowed time as far as the population bomb is concerned, and not very many people seem to be concerned about what we will do when our time runs out. In Alaska, more than in any other place in America, you get the feeling that we have plenty of time left.

I am older now and in the twilight of my years. It is younger people who have to worry about the future. My lifelong dream has been realized. Instead of being a dream, it is now a memory. Someday, I hope to return to Alaska for a longer visit. If this never comes to pass, it doesn't matter, because when I crossed that border into Canada, a part of me stayed behind and will never leave.

CHAPTER 16

Our Environment

By now, I am sure that the reader knows that, like Teddy Roosevelt, I am an environmentalist. I use this label with reluctance because, these days, being one is not politically correct, and to the average American, environmentalists are at best somewhat out of touch with reality and at worst, left-wing socialist nut jobs. To be sure, the political right views environmental issues as red herrings that are being used to impose a socialist agenda on a free and independent capitalist America. Unfortunately, nothing could be further from the truth. Many environmental concerns are not only legitimate but are serious issues that we ignore at our peril.

Our problem, or more appropriately, the situation that keeps us from realizing the nature of our problem, is that we are victims of our past. For man's entire existence on planet Earth, he has been free to do as he pleases without regard to the consequences. Humankind could indiscriminately use what was found in nature; transform it into anything desired without noticeable consequence, and discard anything without concern for the impact that this would have on our environment.

As recently as fifty years ago, industrial corporate stock certificates pictured factories with billowing smokestacks because a smoking chimney was a sign of wealth and prosperity. The accepted panacea of the day for poisonous waste was "dilution is the solution to pollution". In other words, whatever we wanted to dispose of could be dumped into a river or lake, where it would disappear into the environment and no longer be a problem.

We have come a long way from those days, but unfortunately, we have not come far enough. Many people are now sensitized to the need to keep our environment clean, and certainly, there are now many laws in existence to ensure this is the case, but these laws are a Band-Aid on a severed artery. They make us feel better and enable us to think we are doing something to solve the problem, but we are not. The truth of the matter is that we still behave like the world will supply us with an endless flow of raw materials and that it has the capability to absorb an endless flow of waste and pollutants. Only a fool thinks this is the case, but while we pay lip service to environmental concerns, we continue to think and act like fools.

Our problem is that we do too much. We take too much out of the ground, and we discard too much into the environment. Therefore, the key to understanding the root cause of our problem is to ask why. The answer to this question is obvious; we do too much because there are too many of us. The root cause of all our environmental problems is not our doing, but the fact that we have overpopulated our planet. This being the case, it must now be asked how serious the problem is. The answer to this question is a matter of intense debate around the globe, but from where I sit, we are in serious trouble, and all that is necessary to see how bad things are is to open our eyes and look at the record. For example:

Population Growth: The population of the world is presently 7.7 billion human beings, and for the past fifty years, it has increased more rapidly than ever before in history. At the time of Christ, the world population was about 300 million people. By 2050, the world population is expected to increase by another thirty percent and will tally 9.7 billion people. In the year 2100, there is expected to be 11.2 billion souls living on a dead and dying planet.

Mass Extinctions: Mankind is presently causing and witnessing the greatest mass extinction event that has ever occurred in the history of life on our planet. If established trends continue, one-half of all the species that presently exist will be gone in the next several decades. This rate of destruction of life is even greater than the mass extinction caused by a giant meteor collision that occurred sixty-five million years ago and wiped out the dinosaurs. Our present mass extinction is being fueled by human activity, which destroys the habitats of plant and animal life.

Rain Forests Destruction: Rain forests, today, are rapidly disappearing in all areas of the world, and their depletion, without considering anything else, rivals that of the disappearance of the dinosaurs sixty-five million years ago. Every year, Brazil chops down an area of forest the size of the state of Nebraska. In addition to the disappearance of the Amazon basin rain forest, many other forests are being cut down as well. In Indonesia, Zaire, Papua-New Guinea, Malaysia, Burma, the Philippines, Peru, Colombia, Bolivia, and Venezuela, rain forests are disappearing at an alarming rate, and there is no end in sight to the devastation. The primary reason for rainforest demise is their deliberate destruction to make way for farms that will only be used for several years. After that, the exposed soil is depleted of nutrients and will no longer support crops or other plant life or animal life. The farmers responsible for this crime against nature then move on to do the same thing deeper in the rain forest.

Global Warming: Global warming, while still a controversial topic, is being recognized by more and more scientists as a problem that must be dealt with. The evidence in this regard is real and with each passing day, becomes clearer and more compelling. Glaciers throughout the world are receding, the Artic and Antarctic ice packs are disintegrating, global sea levels are rising, world average temperatures are increasing, storms such as hurricanes and cyclones are becoming more numerous and severe, climates are changing, and animals and plant life are shifting their ranges in response to shifts in climate.

Ice Cap melting: Ice sheets at opposite ends of our planet are melting at an ever-increasing rate due to global warming and the overall increase in atmospheric temperatures worldwide. Furthermore, ice sheets spanning thousands of miles in Greenland and Western Antarctica are presently losing approximately 120 cubic miles of ice yearly. This melting of continental ice has resulted in a worldwide rise in sea levels of 11 millimeters since 1992. While this does not seem like much, the trend is alarming because the melting is happening at an ever-increasing rate. Scientists presently predict a sea level rise of 11 to 38 inches by the year 2100. If these predictions come to pass, rising oceans will wreck-havoc on the coastal regions of the world where most people live and where major cities are most prevalent.

Acid Rain: Acid rain is caused by airborne pollutants that acidify falling rain with highly destructive results. Among these is the dying off of trees in the world's forests and reduced agricultural production. Scientists first discovered acid rain in 1852, when the English chemist Robert Agnus invented the term. Acid rain, itself, cannot be seen but its effects are clearly evident. The prime contributors to acid rain are automobiles emissions and coal-burning power plants, but almost all industrial activity makes a contribution. Different regions of the world experience different levels of acid rain, however, so much contributing gases are now being produced that the problem is global and no area of the planet escapes this onslaught.

Solid Waste Disposal: Human activity produces solid waste and far too often this waste is hazardous and dangerous to living things including man. The levels of hazardous waste are continuing to grow throughout the world and this is especially true in developing countries. The more advanced a society is the more hazardous waste it produces, so as third-world countries industrialize, the hazardous waste they produce increases accordingly. Hazardous waste is cumulative in the environment. Once dumped, it stays where it is for many years, and the world's ecosystems are still being affected by waste discarded many years ago. Adding to this problem is the hazardous waste presently being produced and all that will be produced in future years. Included in this waste are spent fuel rods from nuclear power plants which will remain lethal for thousands upon thousands of years.

Water Pollution: Fourteen billion pounds of solid waste and nineteen trillion gallons of liquid waste are dumped in the oceans of the world each year. The oil spill of the Exxon Valdez is a horrible example of this kind of pollution, but what people do not realize is that the total amount of old spilled by the Exxon Valdez was only five percent of the total amount of oil spilled that year. Ocean pollution affects every nation around the world because water movement disperses pollution to every corner of the globe.

Presently, in the center of the Pacific Ocean, there is a huge area where ocean currents concentrate solid waste, and this area looks like a garbage dump. Industrialization is the prime source of water pollution, and as nations become more industrialized, water pollution increases and has a greater impact on fish stocks and the ocean's ability to support life.

Groundwater Depletion: Presently, about 40% of the world's supply of fresh water comes from groundwater. Unfortunately, in many areas of the world, including the Great Plains of the United States, water is pumped from the ground at a faster rate than it can be replenished. Furthermore, as the population increases, the demand for freshwater grows accordingly, intensifying and aggravating the water shortage problem. The inevitable result of over-drawing is increased pumping cost, the deterioration of water quality, land subsidence, saltwater intrusion in coastal areas, and an overall drop in fresh water availability.

Dead Zones: A dead zone is an area in the world's oceans where oxygen depletion causes the death of all living creatures unable to escape from the zone. The size and number of oxygen-deprived "dead zones" throughout the planet have increased steadily since the 1970's and now they number about one hundred fifty. Dead zones are a threat to the world's fisheries and to humans who depend on those fisheries for sustenance. They are caused by excessive nitrogen, which flows into coastal waters from farm runoff, sewage, and emissions from vehicles and factories. In what scientists call a "nitrogen cascade," the chemicals pass, untreated, into our oceans and trigger a proliferation of plankton. In turn, this depletes oxygen in the water. Fish are able to flee from these areas, but slow-moving bottom-dwellers like clams, lobsters, and oysters are less able to escape and die. Dead zones can range from less than a square mile in size, but the largest one is now 45,000 square miles and growing.

Red Tide: For the past several decades, red tide breakouts have been increasing in number and size all around the globe. A red tide is an explosion of one-celled organisms that form a bloom toxic to fish, mammals, and shellfish. Exposure to red tide has sent humans into coughing fits, and blooms in Florida are known to have killed dolphins and manatees. The cause of red tide blooms, which can come in a multitude of colors, is not known with definitive certainty, but research has shown that sewage and agricultural run-off exacerbate the problem.

Fish Stock Depletion: Mankind depends upon the oceans to produce a significant amount of the food it eats. Since the 1950's fish stocks throughout the world have been significantly decreasing, and more and more varieties are being classified as being overexploited or depleted. Currently, only three percent of marine stocks are classified as being underexploited, while twenty-one percent are moderately exploited, which means that present fish stocks could support a modest increase in fishing and harvest levels. However, fifty-two percent are being fished at their maximum biological productivity, and this means they are fully exploited, such that increased fishing would reduce future harvest levels. The remaining twenty-four percent are classified as being overexploited (16%), depleted (7%), or recovering from depletion (1%). Of the top ten food species of fish, seven of them are presently fully exploited or overexploited.

Is the human race truly in peril? In light of all of the above, I fail to understand how anyone can conclude that we do not have a problem, especially when one considers the fact that the world's population is expected to increase by fifty percent in the next fifty years, but the situation is far worse than that. All biological systems, irrespective of whether or not we are talking about a lake, a person, a river, a plant, an area of the planet, or the entire planet, carry on life processes which include ingesting material, using it in some manner, and ejecting unwanted byproducts. Biological systems, by their nature, are resilient and have the ability to ingest varying amounts of pollutants or poisons without harm. However, each biological system has a finite capacity in this regard. There are three stages of pollution evident in biological entities: the green or healthy stage, the yellow or cautionary stage, and the red or lethal stage.

In the green stage of pollution, pollutants are introduced into a biological system and are broken down into harmless chemicals and/or are expelled by the system's natural cleansing processes. The overriding characteristic of this stage is that pollutants are introduced at a rate where there is no net buildup within the system. The cleansing processes function fast enough to handle the influx of unwanted material.

In the yellow stage of pollution, pollutants are introduced into a biological system at such a rate that the cleansing processes cannot cope with the influx, and a backlog of unwanted material begins to accumulate. The overriding characteristic of this stage is that if the rate of ingestion is slowed or stops, the biological system, of its own accord, will return to the green stage, and no irreversible damage has occurred. However, if the influx continues, then this will eventually drive the biological system into the red stage of pollution.

In the red stage of pollution, the yellow stage has persisted for so long that the resulting buildup of pollutants destroys or alters the biological system's natural cleansing processes. The overriding characteristic of this stage is that permanent damage has been done to the system that is irreversible unless someone or something external to the system takes action. The red pollution stage is critical for a biological system because without outside intervention, death is assured.

If a person ingests poison, the correct antidote will cure him. If a lake becomes choked with algae and all life in it dies, the algae can be removed, the water treated, and living things reintroduced. These actions will restore the lake to its original vitality. If a man acts in a timely manner and takes the proper corrective action, he can save almost all troubled biological systems from destruction. However, what if the biological system we are talking about is the world's oceans, or its atmosphere, or the entire planet itself? What will man be able to do to save himself when the entire planet enters the red pollution zone?

No intelligent person with a smattering of knowledge about what is going on in the world today believes that our planet is presently in the green pollution zone. On the other side of the coin, very few people believe our planet is in the red or lethal pollution zone. Therefore, it should be clear that most people would agree that we are in the yellow pollution stage; the real issue is how close are we to the red stage? I think the answer to this question is that we are too close for comfort and that we should be doing everything possible to reverse the direction we are heading. Furthermore, I also believe that if the population of the world doubles in the next fifty years, as predicted, we are doomed. This being the case, what can we do to save ourselves? It may already be too late to do that, but the only hope we have is to radically change how we think and how we behave.

Let's pretend for a moment that this nation has constructed a spaceship to colonize a planet in a distant galaxy, which will take several human lifetimes to reach. The number of people sent on this mission would be limited by the physical space available and the spacecraft's biological ability to sustain its population of interplanetary pilgrims. For survival's sake, the population level of our starship would have to be carefully controlled, and the right to procreate indiscriminately would be suspended. Additional children would only be allowed to replace existing travelers who have died. Obviously, these restrictions would be willingly accepted by those brave enough to make such a dangerous journey, and if not, those who could not live by such rules would not be allowed to go.

The above scenario is hypothetical, but having landed a man on the moon, the possibility of man colonizing other planets is not something that an educated person of today would judge to be impossible. This being the case, it is self-evident that the number of people on the starship would have to be kept under control so as not to overwhelm the craft's environmental and life support systems. If this is so easy to understand and accept in regard to our starship, why is it so hard to understand that we are now at a point on this planet where restrictions on procreation are necessary to ensure our survival? We live on an object we call Earth, and planet Earth, in truth, is nothing more than a spaceship we travel on, not to a far-off planet, but to a questionable and uncertain future.

The huge rock we live on; has everything we need to survive including mechanisms for dealing with pollution. However, there is a finite amount of everything that is here and a limit to how much pollution our world can process. This means that to survive, we have to limit to how many of us are onboard the rock. Technology and the more efficient utilization of resources may be able to increase the sustainable population limit to some degree, but technology also has its limits and even if we do everything in the most efficient manner possible, a limit to how many people can live here will always be there. The undeniable truth is that if we allow too many of us to live on the rock, it will lose its capability of supporting us and we will die. To think this is not the case and that technology will always bail us out, is absurd. The real issue then, is not whether or not the world has a finite capacity to support the doings of man, but at what level of population will we reach the point of no return.

Presently, the world's population is 7.7 billion people. Industrialized nations use the most resources and produce the most pollution. The United States with three percent of the world's population, presently consumes about twenty percent of its resources. This consumption results in a similar percentage contribution to the pollution of our planet. The world is presently in yellow pollution stage and the question is, what stage of pollution will we be in if the other ninety-seven percent of humanity is raised to our standard of living? Is there anyone in their right mind that would hold that this wouldn't put us over the edge?

Scientists have calculated that to be safely in the green pollution zone, with all people enjoying the same standard of living as we have in the United States, world population should be no more that two billion people. Presently we are at three times that number and climbing rapidly. How deep into the yellow pollution zone does being three times over a sustainable level of population put us? Indeed, in consideration of these numbers, isn't it more reasonable to wonder if a population level of six billion people has placed us well into the red pollution zone? After all, aren't we already witnessing the die off of most other forms of life on our planet? Like canaries in a mine, doesn't this tell us something?

As stated previously, I am old and do not have to worry about the answers to these questions. However, people younger than me do and unfortunately for them, people are still debating these issues instead of doing something about them. I started this travelogue by telling you that I thought there were too many people in the world. Pollution issues aside, this is also true because of quality-of-life issues. How good are our lives when we work five days a week, and spend three hours of that same day trying to get to and from work in traffic jams? Is living the good life, hiding in your home or apartment in a major city, because it is unsafe to breathe the air outside? Does life have very much value when it is difficult to find a rural road to drive down without homes lining every stretch of the way?

Beyond any doubt, we are in the yellow or cautionary pollution zone and moving deeper into it. This being the case, it is imperative that we take action now before it is too late. Indeed, if we are truly rational creatures as we so pride ourselves on being, then the prudent thing to have done, was to address the problem when we first passed from the green pollution zone into the yellow one. Granted, no one knows when this occurred, so we did nothing when it happened. However, we now know beyond any doubt that we are over the line. To argue that there is no need for alarm or that we can forgo addressing the problem until we get a little closer to the red zone is absurd. But this is what the "naysayers" would have us do. They argue, there is no need for concern, not all scientists agree with these more "radical assessments", and the best thing to do now is nothing. In other words, they hold that if we ignore the problem, there is no problem or it will go away.

Recall if you will our starship and the interplanetary pilgrims aboard it. Would any of them be listened to by the others if they argued that they should allow more births because the yellow pollution zone was not really something that they should be concerned about. Of course not! If someone onboard the ship held that it was wise to allow pollutants to continually build up on the starship, they would be judged to be insane. Furthermore, if someone aboard the starship actually became pregnant when they weren't supposed to, that pregnancy would be terminated irrespective of the person's wishes. Doesn't this make sense and wouldn't this be the way things would be if our starship was a reality? Please understand that I am only making a point here. I do not believe that this draconian action is necessary to save this planet. However, what is necessary is to realize we have a problem and to educate people about what must be done to solve the problem.

We did not act when we entered the yellow pollution zone, not because we shouldn't have, but because no one realized what was happening. We now know what is happening and this being the case, there are no sound reasons for not taking action. To argue otherwise is lunacy and a death warrant.

About the Author

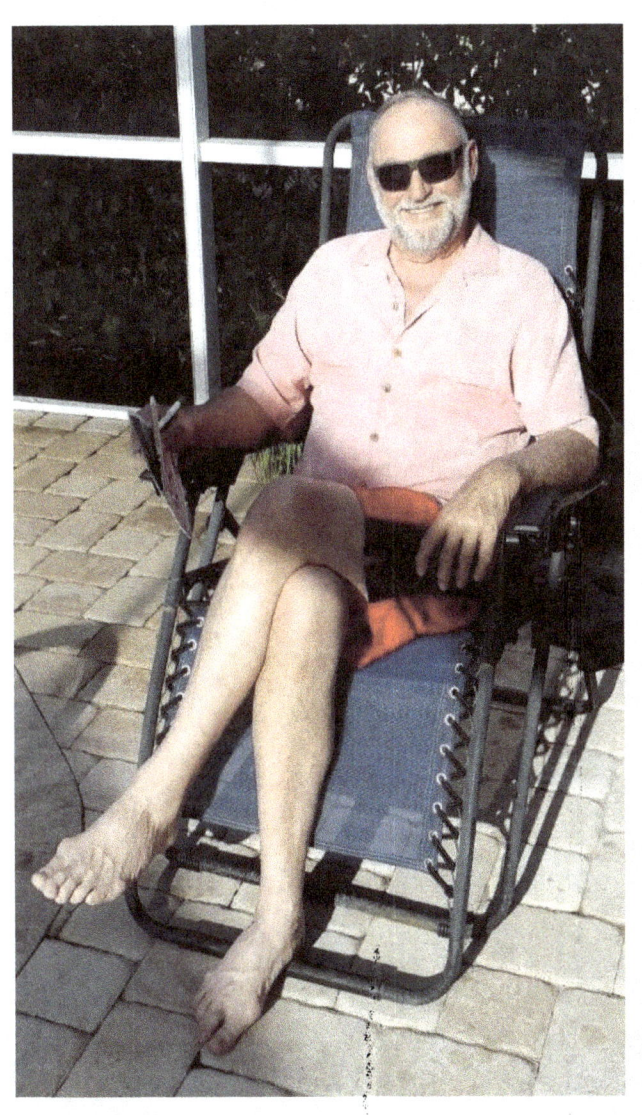

Alan R. Adaschik was raised in Brooklyn, New York. After high school, he became an engineering student at the University of Michigan in its Naval ROTC program and subsequently qualified for Navy flight training. He received his wings as a jet fighter pilot in 1966 and, after completing his tour of duty, earned an MBA from Long Island University. Alan has worked as a flight test conductor for the Grumman Aerospace Corporation, a financial analyst for the Singer Company, a senior financial analyst for Pratt & Whitney Aircraft, and a financial administrator for the City of Fort Lauderdale. Alan is also the author of the newly published book entitled "100 Years of Deception".

ME AND GALE

December

25, 1949

Motor Sport

Jet fighter pilot in 1966

100 Years of Deception: A Blueprint for the Destruction of a Nation

This book uncovers how the 1913 passage of the Federal Reserve Act marked the quiet dismantling of the U.S. Constitution, setting in motion a century of corruption, fabricated histories, and global control. Backed by historical analysis and a call to awaken from complacency, it challenges readers to question official narratives, recognize the forces shaping their lives, and reclaim the principles that once made America a beacon of freedom.

Scan QR Code to visit author's website: